¹³ Blessed are those who find wisdom,
those who gain understanding,

¹⁴ for she is more profitable than silver
and yields better returns than gold.

Proverbs 3:13-14 (NIV)

"Bishop Farr offers some practical and insightful tips that could help clergy and laity engage in fruitful ministry in a variety of contexts. I appreciate him offering this resource as a gift to the church for such a time as this."

Bishop Tracy Smith Malone
East Ohio Conference of the United Methodist Church

"This book needs to be in the hands of every young person entering ministry. Scratch that. It needs to be in the hands of every person in ministry and every lay leader in our churches. For what you have here is true wisdom mined from the real world and decades of fruitful ministry; wisdom that is not only spot-on, but immensely practical and useful. This gift from our Missouri bishop will undoubtedly help you grow as a leader in the local church."

Rev. Ron Watts
Sr. Pastor, La Croix Church, Cape Girardeau, MO

"I have come to expect the practical, the powerful, the pragmatic and the poignant from Bishop Bob Farr. This book is no exception. He writes to equip those who lead the church because he loves the church. He is a mentor who speaks with authority because he has led effective ministry at every level. Whether you engage this book as a matter of personal reflection or in a small group setting, your time and energy will be rewarded."

Rev. Shane L. Bishop
Sr. Pastor Christ Church , Fairview Heights, Illinois

"In the midst of the whirlwind of ministry, the obvious isn't always apparent. Especially in these times, it good to be reminded by a wise friend about what's important; about where to focus. Bishop Farr has been that wise friend for me and countless others and has packed so much of that into bite-sized chapters that don't add to the overwhelm. *Obvious Wisdom* will be a treasured gift for those who are seeking to make a difference for Jesus without losing their mind."

Christie Latona
Director of Connectional Ministries of the Baltimore-Washington Conference

"*Obvious Wisdom* offers important insight into critical pastoral wisdom. Much like a baseball team going to spring training to practice skills it already knows, *Obvious Wisdom* shares perceptive reminders for effective ministry that all pastors need. It should be used as an important resource for pastors of all ages and levels of experience to periodically read or re-read a pertinent chapter to guide their ministry into greater pastoral effectiveness."

Bishop Mike Lowry
Resident Bishop of The Central Texas Conference of the United Methodists Church

Obvious Wisdom

52 tips for effective ministry

by Bishop Bob Farr

Market
Square
BOOKS

Obvious Wisdom
52 tips for effective ministry

by Bishop Bob Farr

©2018 Market Square Publishing Company, LLC.
books@marketsquarebooks.com
P.O. Box 23664 Knoxville, Tennessee 37933

ISBN: 978-1-7323092-0-3

Library of Congress: 2018942996

Printed and Bound in the United States of America

Editors: Kevin Slimp & Kristin Lighter
Design by Earl Goodman
Cover by Lauren Miers

Table of Contents

Foreword

I met Bob Farr more than 30 years before he was elected "Bishop Farr," when we were both youth directors at congregations in the North Texas Conference of the United Methodist Church.

Along with our mutual friend, Fred Baum, who worked with youth at a nearby United Methodist Church, we prayed together, directed camps together, led youth rallies together, held overnighters together and spent many hours attempting to perfect our craft before parting ways, moving on to ministries in Missouri, Arizona and Florida.

When Bishop Farr and I first began to discuss the possibility of publishing this book, he could hardly control his enthusiasm. I felt like I was talking to the same "Bob" I knew all those years ago, as he expressed his hope to ease the path for others who are sure to encounter many of the same obstacles he has faced over these almost-forty years in ministry.

This book is Bishop Farr's attempt to share some of the "obvious wisdom" he has obtained as he approaches 40 years in ministry. Whether you read the book from cover to cover, or read one chapter each week, our prayer is that your path will be made more clear by the words contained within.

Kevin Slimp, Publisher

Acknowledgments

I am deeply indebted to my mentors, clergy and lay colleagues who over the years have stopped me with obvious wisdoms from doing stupid. Those wisdoms and tips weren't so obvious to an inexperienced young pastor at the time. Thank you! This book is to honor you and hopefully help some new colleagues to be as fruitful as possible in their ministry.

I am thankful for the dedicated help of the Director of Connectional Ministries, Kim Jenne and my Executive Assistant, Catherine Turner in writing this book. Thank you!

I am so thankful to my spouse, Susan Farr for putting up with and listening to all my stuff through the 40 years of marriage and ministry. She has always been and always will remain my most important partner in ministry. Thank you! I love you, Susan.

Introduction

I was two weeks into my first full-time pastoral assignment at Randolph Memorial, a United Methodist Church located in old Kansas City suburbia when Rev. Dr. Harold Dodds of Country Club UMC walked into my little office.

The name Rev. Dodds didn't mean much to me at the time, but Country Club did. Thirty years ago, in 1985, Country Club UMC was a high steeple church in a very moneyed neighborhood on the Plaza. I couldn't imagine why the senior pastor was sitting across from me. Thankfully, I did not ask aloud the question on my mind, "Why are you here?" But, after the typical niceties, he helped me answer that question in short order. He said, "Bob, we need each other." I blurted out, "For what?" I operated out of a 'Methodist-lone wolf' perspective of ministry. I could not imagine why in the world I would need an old pastor in my life, let alone one from Country Club which was so different from my ministerial setting.

"Here's the deal," Dodd said. "You need a mentor because you are going to make some really dumb mistakes if you don't have someone to talk to and who might be willing to say, 'you might want to think about that before you do it'." It almost offended me. I was 25, recently graduated from seminary and thought I had it all figured out. Perhaps the look on my face gave it away because he said, "And I need you. I have been in ministry for a long time. I perceive that you have a lot of new ideas about ministry. I haven't had a new idea in a while. You could help me with some new ideas. Could we have a mutual relationship here? I could help you think through some things and you can give me a new idea or two. I'll even buy lunch once a week."

Sold.

That conversation began a 15-year friendship that spanned two appointments. He gave me tips about ministry that I continue to practice today. They were not grandiose ideas. Most of his wisdom were little practices for self-care or thoughts on managing the rigors of a busy parish life. But, while the ideas were not ingenious, they were often life-changing practices that shaped my ministry and my leadership.

Harold passed away a few years ago. I was very lucky to have met him and that my confident and brash 25-year-old self accepted his invitation to begin a collegial friendship. He brought a lot of experience to the table. He gave me perspective. He was a lot more cautious than I was, and he probably saved me from some painful mistakes. The gift that Harold gave me is one that I'd like to pass along. This book is filled with lessons learned along a 40-year career in ministry. Many of these ideas are not original or novel. Some of them are exactly the suggestions that Harold offered me so long ago.

When I started my pastoral ministry in 1978, in a small two-room open country church outside Harrisonville, Missouri, I had no idea what would become of the next 40 years. Fact is, I very rarely gave it any thought at all. At eighteen, I was simply trying to make it through one college semester after another, write a 10-minute sermon every seven days, and make enough money to put gas in my car to carry me and my girlfriend around Cass County back and forth to Warrensburg. In the midst of it all, I was also trying to convince myself that becoming a pastor might very well be my vocational future.

The time and effort needed to become an ordained elder in the United Methodist Church seemed like an unlikely possibility given my struggles with college-level coursework and navigating the early days of my first appointment. At 18 and newly licensed to preach, I was always the youngest pastor, oftentimes the youngest person, in the room. If you asked me, I would have told you I thought I was pretty good at preaching, but I had absolutely no idea what I was doing. My first congregation didn't hesitate to tell me so. I kept waiting for the District Superintendent to tell me, "Thanks, but no thanks," but each week, I drove to Harrisonville, MO to preach to a small group of faithful women and men who tolerated me pontificating on scripture in front of them.

Forty years later, those early days in my first year as a Bishop in the United Methodist Church, have often come to mind and I wondered how it all came to pass. The 18-year-old version of me would have never believed my 58-year-old future self. Only a grace-filled God could have mapped out this plan.

My ministry has been exciting, frustrating, fun, hard, interesting and filled with so many good, faithful people and close-knitted relationships that I could not have possibly dreamed it into existence. I hope my ministry has been purposeful and useful to the kingdom of God. I hope lives have been changed for the better. I truly hope forgiveness will be extended for those times when I may have hurt more than helped.

Over the course of 40 years, I was privileged to pastor
six different congregations. The churches were as diverse as
they could be, ranging in size from 25 people to 1,200 people,
open-country to urban and suburban settings, three-point
charge to single status with an extensive paid staff. I was
privileged to plant a church and grow something from nothing, and lead the relocation of a growing church to a more
visible highway location in the growing business district
of the community. To this day, I view serving as pastor to
a community the highest privilege there is in life. I spent
the last 10 years of my ministry in judicatory work: first as
the Director of Congregational Excellence for the Missouri
Conference, and now as a Bishop in my second year.

People have asked me for another book and I have
wondered what I would write that has not already been said
or written. What wisdom, if any, could I share from a varied
career in local church ministry? I have considered how often
the Church across the centuries seemed to be dying and yet
lived to see an even brighter day. I have thought of the untold
men and women who labored for a people they would never
know and for results they would not see. I've thought about
the small, unlikely band of leaders and followers that made
up the early church movement.

In the midst of tyrannical powers and persecution,
their future seemed sure to be stamped out. Yet, their faith
sparked a fire that spread throughout the entire world and
continues to burn today. I reflected on the heroes of early
American Methodism: John Wesley, Francis Asbury, Captain
Thomas Webb, Barbara Heck, Harry Hosier, Mary Bosan-
quet, Richard Allen and Sarah Crosby. Their religious movement expanded from 61,351 members, 272 itinerant pastors
and one bishop in 1799 to 312,540 members, 1,226 preachers

and five bishops by 1824; an increase of 400 percent![1] Today, I am a bishop in the same Methodist movement that has been in steady decline for over 50 years. Despite this national trend, my own experience in every congregation I served was one of growth.

Through some combination of God's blessing, gifted laity leaders and grace, we managed to buck the trend of decline and I count the new people who came to know Jesus as one of the greatest blessings of my life. I recalled my travels to dozens of congregations over the last 10 years where the embers of the Holy Spirit seemed to have cooled. Other congregations I worked with had rekindled the spark and began a new chapter of fruitful ministry that can only be explained as the Holy Spirit-guiding the labors of the pastor and people of faith.

What could I say that would be helpful in such a time as this? I've asked my wife of 38 years, Susan, over and over what I might share that could be helpful or practical for pastors and their families. As a Bishop of the Church, what could I say that might help our pastors and churches through this time of great transition? I have thought about where the Church in the United States and the global world finds itself in the 21st century. What are my hopes for the future of the Church in a post-modern, post-Christian world?

People ask me over and over, "tell your stories," or "share your Farr-isms." This, in itself, is funny to me. While my whole staff can list off one Farr-ism after another, I tell them all the time, I don't realize I'm saying a Farr-ism, that's just me talking. I have come to learn that what they mean is they want me to share my common sense approach which I

1 John H. Wigger *American Saint: Francis Asbury and the Methodist,* Oxford University Press (2009)

always try to infuse with a little humor and hopefulness. I've come to find that those Farr-isms, what I call here "simple wisdom," might serve as an encouragement to others who are doing the work that I have spent the greatest part of my life loving. Consider the following pages lessons learned over a lifetime of ministry. So many of them I wish I had learned earlier in my ministry. It may have saved me from heart-ache and disappointment. It certainly would have saved my congregations from me!

In the same way that Rev. Dr. Harold Dodds, offered me wisdom early in my career, I offer this book as some practi-cal advice for leaders of local churches. We don't get a whole lot of do-overs in this life, but if I were to do it all over again, I would work harder to master these 52 practices. This is certainly not a finite list. Each day, especially in my new work, I learn lessons that inform the leader I am becoming and the leader I hope to be one day. I pray that you might discover in this shared wisdom areas where you might expe-rience growth in your own leadership style.

In Christ,

Bishop Robert "Bob" Farr

CHAPTER 1

I Would Be Excited

I would be excited. Of course, I'd be more excited about some things than others. I would go to each church I am sent with a boatload of enthusiasm. We can spend our entire life looking for greener pastures or we can decide to help turn the pasture we are already in, green.

I never received a church appointment that I wanted or thought I deserved. Yet, in six different assignments, each church turned out to be life-changing. Each spring when the phone rang from a District Superintendent or Bishop calling to share where they thought I should go, I always thought that the Cabinet had lost their minds. They couldn't possibly be right! Yet, each assignment turned out to be right where I needed to be for that season of my life. Either I had a gift or skill-set that the church needed or the church offered a ministry opportunity that I needed to explore or master. In some cases, it was both.

In the Missouri Conference, retiring clergy give a short reflection on their ministry. David Norbury retired in 2012 after 45 plus years in ministry and approximately 12 churches. In his statement, he shared after each church, saying, "And it was the best appointment I ever had." I think David had the right attitude. Looking back, I don't regret any of my church appointments. Now, there were times when

I was ready to give the pastorate back to the Bishop. There were some Sunday evenings and Monday mornings when driving a school bus full of cats would have been easier than what I was going through at the moment. Still, nothing else I have ever done has been as life-fulfilling as the pastoral ministry.

You might ask, "Why did you become a bishop?" As with local church ministry, there have been some Sunday nights and Monday mornings over the past year when I have asked myself the same question. The answer? Mixed reasons. If I'm totally honest, it flattered my ego. It is a supreme challenge in our profession. It offers tremendous possibilities for service and influence. It offers me the chance to make a difference in ministry on a larger scale.

I thought I could influence pastors and churches for the better. I thought it was time to turn a page and lead from a different position. I consider the work I am doing as a multiplication of influence. It is a privileged position whereby my influence and power can be used to help shape future leaders and thereby the future of the Church.

Within this privileged position, I am reminded daily as I do pastoral care for pastors, that, despite a title change, I remain a pastor who happens to be a bishop. When people asked me what I do, I typically respond, "I'm a pastor in the United Methodist Church." When they ask where my church is, I respond, "I'm a bishop."

After two years into the role, I'm still excited about the possibilities. The key to success is to approach every church or position in ministry we receive with enthusiasm. The key to life is approaching every day looking for the blessings rather than the negatives. In the midst of our hardest times in ministries – and there will be days, weeks, even seasons of hard ministry – it is even more important to develop a regular practice of gratitude and thanksgiving. This spiritual discipline pulls the focus off ourselves to allow us to see what God is doing with and for us, even when life is challenging.

I know some pastors have not found ministry as life-fulfilling as I have. I also know that not every minister should be a pastor. If you are a pastor who has found that ministry is not life-fulfilling, I would encourage you to discover another way to live out your baptism. Get out before it is too late for the sake of your own soul. Don't waste your life where you are not serving where you should. God will provide many other ways for you to be in ministry.

As for me, I would receive every church with excitement believing this is the best church since sliced bread; you want to be there forever and will work at it like you are going to be there forever. People know the difference. They know when you have planted roots and when you're just passing through.

The church is the hope of the world. Jesus is our salvation, but the church is God's chosen instrument to bring hope to a broken world. Being a pastor of that church is the most important work in the world. It is no bed of roses and not the easiest career we could choose. There are thorns along the way and you are going to bleed every once in a while. When you are sharing in Christ's work, you share in Christ's suffering and in Christ's joy. Most of it is joy!

I would be excited.

CHAPTER 2

Remember to Pray

I would remember to pray. The easiest place to lose Jesus is working inside the Church. If I were back inside the local church again, I would be more purposeful in my prayer routine. Looking back, I probably approached personal prayer in the same manner often attributed to Abraham Lincoln, "...driven many times upon my knees by the overwhelming conviction that I had nowhere else to go."[2] Especially early in my ministry, I confess that having regular, personal prayer time didn't happen within the confines of my week. I relied on the public praying I led, and there was plenty of opportunities for that. If you are not careful, you will think that public prayer within worship and church meetings covers all of your prayer needs. It does not. In fact, it is a convenient mask for a stagnant spiritual life. I should know. Too often, I recited my Sunday-printed prayers and performed public prayers on behalf of a congregation of people, all the while lacking a personal dialogue and a deepening relationship with the Lord.

Hindsight is truly 20/20. In reflection, I can point to my lack of spiritual life many times over my 40-year journey. In

---

2 Whether or not Lincoln actually said this is under dispute by Lincoln scholars. President Obama referenced the 16th President in conjunction with this quote during the 2012 Democratic National Convention.

fact, it is my Achilles' heel. I remember time and time again, while standing at the front door after worship, people would ask me to pray for something in their life. I would assure them I would pray, only to forget the conversation by lunch. One day, a lady called me on Sunday evening to update me on her health situation and thanked me for my prayers. I could not remember what she had shared with me earlier in the day. I hung up the phone and cried. I was faking it. I was entrusted with a sacred privilege of helping to carry the prayer burdens for a group of people and was derelict in my duty. Even more, I began to wonder what my ministry might begin to look like if it was grounded, truly grounded, in the spirit of the Lord. I had discovered, that as a young white man with a great deal of privilege and a strong work ethic, I could accomplish a great deal simply on my own gumption and resourcefulness. How long could that possibly last? What more was possible if I admitted that I could not do without the help of God?

From that day forward, I wrote down each request given to me and set time aside to, at the very least, pray for the requests given to me. That dedicated time in prayer on behalf of others taught me how to begin a conversation of my own with the Lord. For as much time as I had spent growing up in the Church, I had never learned to develop a disciplined approach to prayer. I saw the connection in my own spiritual growth.

If I were a pastor again, I would structure my personal prayer time and pray. I would protect that time against the multitude of excuses and good causes that would attempt to disrupt this routine. And believe me, the onslaught against this time is constant. I would set aside time every day. I would create a special place for this prayer time. Currently, my space is my back porch overlooking the woods in my backyard. I've learned to make a list of prayer requests.

In addition, I have learned how to incorporate prayer time throughout the busyness of the day. Rather than let my mind wander, I've learned how to pray in the silence of my walk around my neighborhood. I have learned that drive time can be quiet time, prayer time; even with my eyes open. I've learned to pray scripture. I have discovered how to pray written prayers, learning that the words of other prayers often give me the language to express my own feelings or thoughts.

I've learned to pray every day for my wife, Susan, our children and our grandchildren. I have a special habit of praying for our two adult children during my morning commute. I've learned to pray the Psalms, and pray for those persons I do not like and those who do not like me. My prayers are not complicated, poetic or long. They don't need to be. My morning prayers typically cover the following areas:

- **Thank you for...**

- **Forgive me for...**

- **Come, Holy Spirit...**

If I were a pastor again, I would deepen my prayer life. I would open myself to the Holy Spirit and let a little awe and mystery into my life. I would let loose of the steering wheel of my life and allow God to do more of the driving. This continues to be a hard lesson for me. I have trouble trusting my car's GPS; and I can see it in front me. Letting a God I cannot see serve as my life's GPS is decidedly more difficult. I continue to learn Paul's admonition to Christians that "We fix our eyes not on what is seen, but on what is unseen, since what is seen is temporary, but what is unseen is eternal" (2 Cor. 4:18 [NIV]).

I think back over the years and wonder at my inadequacy at letting God be God in my life. I wonder at the grace God has offered me in the midst of my lack of humility and arrogance. I could no longer imagine my parish ministry – with all its complexities, heartbreaks, wounds and sin – without imagining a vibrant prayer life. I think of an old hymn that talks about grace upon grace. Thank God for God's grace, even in my inadequate prayer life and I give thanks and ask for forgiveness even as I ask for more Holy Spirit. Come, Holy Spirit, Come!

I would remember to pray.

— CHAPTER 3 —

Love People Anyway

I would love people anyway. We have all read "Love your enemies and pray for those who persecute you," (Matt. 5:44) and wondered, "How in the world am I supposed to do that?!" There have been a few days of pastoral ministry that I thought, "If this is how my friends treat me, I'd rather meet my enemies." Despite this, I would try like crazy to love people anyway! One of my favorite country songs, "People are Crazy" contains the refrain: "God is great, beer is good, and people are crazy."[3] I would love people anyway. I would love them in spite of their craziness but because of it.

The human spirit is something. It is hard to fathom what humans have done to one another over the course of human history and what they continue to do to one another. If you are in a profession that deals with people for any length of time, you will need a great capacity to deal with pain and disappointment. I would love people anyway. On the other hand, it is incredible what wonderfully good things humans can and will do for other humans. Fred Rogers, the popular public television personality and Presbyterian minister, often told the story about when he was a boy and would see scary things on the news: "My mother would say to me, 'Look for the helpers. You will always find people who are

---

3 Currington, Billy. *Little Bit of Everything.* Mercury Nashville, 2008, compact disc.

helping.'"[4] Like Rev. Rogers, I am always comforted by the realization that there continue to be so many caring people in this world. If you work with the public for very long, you will serve as a witness to the incredibly decent and noble things humans do for one another each and every day. I would love people anyway.

We are in the people business. If you are apt to say, "I don't care for people much," and you're in paid ministry, you need to look for a different job. This work is about people. The Apostle Paul wrote to the church in Corinth and reminded them that God gave us the task of making others his friends: "Christ changed us from enemies into his friends and gave us the task of making others his friends also" (2 Cor. 5:18 [GNT]). "Become friends with God; God's already a friend with you" (2 Cor. 5:18 [MSG]). Because of that, I would love people anyway.

One of the things I've learned along the way I wish I had known earlier is that we don't know what else is going on in a person's life that might make them appear a "little crazy" to us at the moment. We all have a little crazy lurking just below the surface of our lives. That's the point of Billy Currington's song. We're people, too. I believe this is why Jesus prayed for the crowd gathered below the cross, "Father, forgive them, for they do not know what they are doing" (Luke 23:34). I would love people anyway. Try it. Loving others helps you love the parts about yourself you don't care for. It helps you discover how to live out the commandment to "Love your neighbor as yourself" (Matt. 22:39).

I would love people anyway.

---

4 *Helping Children with Scary News: Helping Children Deal with Tragic Events in the News* PBS.org, PBSParents. Last modified, 22 December 22, 2017, http://www.pbs.org/parents/rogers/special/scarynews-thoughts.html.

CHAPTER 4

Delegate More

I would delegate more. More times than I would like to admit, I robbed others of the chance to demonstrate and offer their gifts. When pastors try to do too much for those in their pews and the mission field, we enable all kinds of bad behavior; and our communities become less fruitful than they might otherwise have been.

This is probably the greatest struggle I see in other leaders. The problem boils down to trading short-term pain for long-term ineffectiveness. This lesson took me longer to learn than it probably should have. It was just easier to do it myself than try to find and trust someone else to do the task that was pressing upon me at the present moment. When we make the trade, we lessen someone else's gifts for the future and stunt our community's growth. We fail in our apostleship.

When I started at Church of the Shepherd in St. Charles, I essentially designed the worship service, as well as planned the sermon, all by myself. I even practiced a "plug and play" approach with the church musicians, giving them blanks in the service bulletin to fill in. Over the course of my time there, we built together a team of gifted people for a variety of worship tasks, including designing and planning, and it absolutely expanded our capacity to do ministry. During that season of ministry, I experienced some of the best worship of my life because more voices provided more creativity. My sermons got better, I got better feedback to help build upon.

Additionally, my workload changed and it freed me up to focus on sermon delivery and other church visioning work. I spent 25 years of ministry doing worship my way, without any input from other leaders. I wish I had managed the short term pain of teaching others and leading them to step into this role. I would have experience better worship for a longer period of time.

As pastors, our role is to set the example, model excellence and hand the role off to another disciple. Once I realized it was a discipleship issue, I never asked anyone to do something I was not willing to do and had already done. However, pastors should not be the congregation's nursemaid. We are to help others discover their gifts for the betterment of the church. We are facilitators of the gifts of the body of the church (1 Cor. 12). One of the things I tried to do was to set up a process of helping people believe in themselves and recognize their own potential. This is a critical part of the discipleship pathway for Christians. Helping people name their own call to ministry and see their place in the kingdom of God is difficult work. Trust me, sometimes it *is* just easier to do yourself. You will be tempted time and time again. I would still let others do it. If you want to see a church completely disabled, prevented from truly being the Church, just do everything for them all the time. If you need to be liked all the time, just do it all. However, you will disable the church and do a disservice to the body of Christ and those individuals.

A fruitful pastor shows confidence in others and learns to trust and delegate. Part of trust is relinquishing control.

Once you hand something over to someone, support them, guide them, give them clear expectations, but realize they won't complete the task like you would. That's okay. If you are a perfectionist, as you implement this discipleship process, you will likely experience pain around surrendering. This in itself can be an act of obedience, trusting that the Holy Spirit has equipped the community for the work of the Church, "The manifestation of the Spirit is given for the common good" (1 Cor. 12:7).

Sometimes you hand off a project out of necessity as things begin to grow, but also because you realize that your gifts are limiting the ministry. At one of my churches, I had to let go of hospital visitation. The size of the congregation was making it impossible for one pastor to do anything other than that. I had to turn it over to a team. Shortly thereafter, I discovered that my associate pastor led that ministry far better than I ever did. I'm a great pastor in a crisis but Carol was brilliant for the long haul. She loved and cared for those families through illness, disease and end of life processes. I am thankful that in turning over this ministry to gifted leaders, the ministry expanded and deepened. In the case of visitation or congregational care ministry, if you move to a team approach, learn to resist sweeping in at the end and presiding at the funeral.

This undercuts the entire ministry and decapitates the leader of that ministry. It does a disservice to the ministry of the laity and the associates. I had to let go of those funerals. One year, our church celebrated 23 funerals. I conducted three. The person who has been carrying the ball on care of the family needs to finish the work. I would always attend the funerals and be at the front door greeting the family as they arrived. I would offer my service to the associate pastor or lay leader and say yes to what they needed from me. I had to let go of leading in this particular way and let others do it differently than I would have. It multiplied our ministry and allowed other leaders to live out their gifts more fully.

The Church is a servant-led organization. Its long-term future is best when you have identified, nurtured and delegated the work to the laity of your congregation. When you pass the baton to a new incoming pastor with dozens of well-trained, spiritually-centered leaders at their disposal you can claim a successful ministry. When all ministry depends only on the pastor, everything stops when that pastor retires, takes a vacation or is assigned to a different church. Your work ultimately fails no matter how good it looks at the moment.

I would delegate more.

— CHAPTER 5 —

Stand For Something

If I were a local pastor again, I would find my voice and offer it for the good of the community and the world. This means putting a stake in the ground and taking a stand. Wishy-washy people who try to please and make everyone happy seldom end up pleasing anyone or having anyone like them. On the other hand, if you try to force what you believe on people all the time, you will not have a very fruitful ministry.

I would stand for something because as Chesterton said, "A dead thing can go with the stream, but only a living thing can go against it."[5] Even a dead fish can float downstream. Open your mouth and say something if you think it needs to be said. Remember, you could be wrong. Standing for something is also about discovering your purpose and finding your voice. Know your purpose.

Use your gifts to that end. Again, remember not everyone must follow the same path. God creates human beings each with their own fingerprint; no two are alike. I like to think it's because God appreciates diversity that our creation is filled with such variety. Find your voice, but be wary you don't displace another voice in the process.

---

[5] G.K. Chesterton, *The Everlasting Man*.

It's a tightrope leaders have to walk: standing on principles on which you won't yield while not forcing everyone
you lead to tread the same path as you. People have often
commented that I'm a straightforward kind of guy. I take
that as a compliment.

It's not always meant as one. I am keenly aware that my
unyielding principles and all my ideas about transformational leadership have the potential to leave bodies in my
wake if I'm not careful. That's not helpful to fruitful pastoral
ministry.

When you're a straight shooter sometimes truthfulness
can come without any grace. Truthfulness without grace
is just being mean. I've done that plenty of times and it is
never a pretty sight. However, grace without truthfulness is
cheap theology and a lie that does not honor God.

Sometimes taking a stand is hard. It can result in pain.
I certainly have some scars from these stands in my own
ministry. One particular instance stands out to me. At one
point in Grace UMC's early ministry we began thinking
about a possible new church start at Lone Jack. The thought
of "dividing" did not go over well with my leadership team
despite the interest and support of worshipers who lived in
Lone Jack. For many of our leaders, they had fallen in love
with our little group.

Instead of multiplication of ministry, they saw planting as division and subtraction of friends. One of our most
committed leaders was incensed by my approach and in
the midst of a very contentious leader meeting gave me an
emotional ultimatum, "You're telling me that you would
choose this decision to go to Lone Jack over our friendship?"

I lost 30 people that day because of my response. I took a
stand on my call to ministry and everything I believe about

evangelism and ministry. I still don't regret making the decision. Some of my leaders could not imagine me choosing the mission of the church over their desire to create a comfortable circle of friends. In hindsight, I have begun to see this as a conflict of preference, not theology or politics. We had begun feeling the growing pains of becoming a 500-person church. I had to take a stand on the mission of the church or the preferences of people I loved.

Sometimes the stands are on smaller issues than planting a second site. It could be about moving from a narthex to a gathering space, style of worship or the times of worship. I once lost 50 people starting a contemporary service because 50 people couldn't imagine worshiping at a different time on Sunday morning. Our expansion of ministry exponentially reached beyond the 50 people who left. Sometimes stands are worth it. Still, they do come with battle scars.

Every person needs to know their plumb line, their yardstick, their values and rocks they stand on. Be careful, your rock could become your stumbling block. It is best to lead people to the place you want them to be rather than push them from behind. Moving people is like herding cats. Cats don't herd; they have to be coaxed or coerced.

One of the great lessons of my career has been in learning that I may not be right. I may arrive in heaven and have Jesus say to me, "You didn't get it right." I am counting on that even then, God will cover me with grace anyway. One of my mantras in my new role has been to remind myself that even when I'm convinced I'm right, to say, "But I could be wrong."

Try it sometime. When you are taking a stand, start with, "I could be wrong, but I believe this is what I am being called to offer as leader of our community." You may discover that in finding your voice, you empower others to find theirs.

I would stand for something.

—— CHAPTER 6 ——

Practice Practices

I would practice three things; okay, four specific things that can apply to the whole of one's life and ministry. And, I would seek to encourage the members of my congregation to do the same. I would strive to practice what United Methodists call John Wesley's General Rules. For the purposes of this writing, I use Bishop Rueben P. Job's language from *Three Simple Rules: A Wesleyan Way of Living*:

- **Do no harm.**

- **Do all the good you can.**

- **Stay in love with God.**

These three simple practices offer a blueprint for a faithful life. I would top off these practices with Wesley's maxim on money:

Earn all you can, save all you can and give all you can.[6]

I believe these four practices can affect a life of discipleship in very positive ways. It offers a compass with which to navigate the map of one's life. Throughout my ministry I

---

6 John Wesley, "The Use of Money" (Sermon 50) in *John Wesley's Sermons: An Anthology. ed. Albert C. Outler and Richard P. Heitzenrater* (Nashville: Abingdon Press, 1991), 347-357.

have tried to practice these things. I have taught them and preached about them. If the church is to find relevance, it's people will have to find renewal in their spiritual life. I think Wesley designed his confessional bands and transformational class meetings (small groups) around these four rules because he had discovered, through his Methodist society during his time at Oxford University, that the practices have the power to change our lives.

Those first three rules are the general rules of a Methodist. They are easier said than done. I have been astonished that in every congregation I've served, people seem to know nothing about them. It's a shame, because they were formative to the early Methodist movement. Every week people in the class meeting reviewed their relationship with Christ by asking one another about the three rules. Wesley added the fourth as a principle more than a rule for accountability related to their weekly commitment to give aid to the poor in their communities.

This fourth axiom is a "redeem and rise" strategy that helped create the middle class of America. Wesley did not believe people had to be stuck where they were socially. They could improve their "lot in life," so to speak. This was a highly radical notion developed in British society where the entire United Kingdom was built with a very structured socio-economic class system. This principle flourished in an American society unencumbered by a heritage of ancestral wealth and aristocracy. Can you imagine where we would be if people actually followed this principle today? Our savings rate would skyrocket, our charitable giving would skyrocket and people's lives would improve. Wesley was a "both/and" kind of guy. He was interested in deepening personal piety while improving the well-being of the community.

Wesley was often criticized for a theology of works' righteousness. Today, prosperity preachers can misunderstand a set of practices like the General Rules as a guarantee to the prevention of suffering or the surefire assurance of financial and social success. This is a misunderstanding of Wesley. He believed that practice shaped people into the people God would have them to be. Our practices, including our practices around money, reflect our souls; Jesus taught, "Where your treasure is, there your heart will be also" (Matt. 6:210. I am a practical guy. I believe in practices. One of the important lessons I learned from my predecessor and bishop, Robert Schnase, was the importance of practices to shape and guide a congregation. His work on *The Five Practices of Fruitful Congregations* was a key contributor to transformation in the Missouri Conference, as well as the broader connectional Church. Grace cannot be earned through anything that we do or say, but I'm with Francis Asbury, "We should so work as if we were to be saved by our works; and so rely on Jesus Christ, as if we did no works." [7]

If I were a pastor again, I would commit to teaching and preaching about these principles over and over. I would commit my life to these practices. I believe it would change our spiritual lives. If were are going to have another Great Awakening, we will need to have a multitude of personal spiritual awakenings first. Do no harm. Do all the good you can. Stay in love with God. Earn all you can, save all you can and give all you can. May it be so.

I would practice Practices.

---

7 Francis Asbury *The Journal of Rev. Francis Asbury, Bishop of The United Methodist Episcopal Church: From August 7, 1771 to December 7, 1815* p.231

CHAPTER 7

Create More Space for God

I would create more space for God. As I have said previously, one of the easiest places in the world to lose God is working inside the church. This might sound crazy, I know. With all the godly symbols around, it can lure us into thinking the symbols are God's presence and that just by simply being there, God is automatically infused into your life.

You can be lulled into thinking that no further time or practice is needed to come into the presence of God. This for me, could not be farther from the truth. Young people are sometimes sent to seminary with the caution, "Don't lose your Jesus!" We all have heard the old saying, "I lost my religion," or "She has lost her religion" as southern slang for losing our tempers.

When you're working in the church, for the church, and with the church, you can lose your religion or faith in a flash. I don't care how dedicated or genuinely devout a person you are, when you get so religiously busy, you are at risk to lose your religion or faith.

If I were back in the saddle of pastoral ministry again, I would create more space to practice the spiritual disciplines that deepen my love for God and others. Know that religious busyness can mask an emptiness that leads to resentment and ultimately burnout: "I have nothing left to share" or "My tank is empty."

I would create space for God. This means a special place and time to pray, to listen and be silent. Set aside a time to read the Bible not for sermon preparation but for no other reason than to spend time in the Word. Set aside time for Bible study that you do not lead. Set aside time to have conversations on spiritual matters with a trusted friend or spiritual director.

Be in covenant with colleagues where you can confess and hold one another accountable. Set aside time to think and read, read, read. Read more than solely spiritual stuff.

If you are not careful, your love for God will slip away bit by bit because of business here and there. In a recent movie, *Lady Bird*, the main character's favorite nun, Sister Sarah Joan (played by Lois Smith), suggests that there is a relationship between love and attention or, perhaps, they are the same thing.

Just like love can slip away in a marriage without attention, our love for God will slip away from us. When that happens as a pastor, our vocation goes from a called vocation, to a job! So, if I were to be someone's pastor again, I would create space for God.

Creating space for God within your daily activities is part of the discipline that comes with discipleship. Admittedly, there are seasons of ministry in which more space can be made. Sometimes life in the parish is chaotic and uneven (i.e., a month with 6 funerals; that happened one time in a church I served).

A regular rhythm of space for God can account for

seasons and periods of busyness. I have heard a rule of thumb of practicing time with God as one hour a day (daily prayer), one day a week (Sabbath) and one weekend a month (2-day retreat). Spiritual life is not a smooth assent to God. Rather, it is filled with hills and valleys, mountain top experiences and periods of desert. It will become all desert if one does not create space for God. God is always with us, no matter what (Rom. 8:38-39).

Part of the life of faith is acknowledging the dual competing forces of presence and absence of God. It's like the old story of two people in love seated in their car's front seat. In the initial days, weeks and months of romance, they are snuggled up close to one another. Over time, they find themselves riding in the front seat farther and farther apart.

The passenger says to the other, "Why did you move over?" The one in the driver's seat says, "I'm not the one who moved over." God never moves over. We do; usually under the guise of not enough time. God is often the first thing we cut from our busy schedules. The first stumbling block to a deeper spiritual life is busyness.

God's presence within us, even before we acknowledge it, is the prevenient grace Wesley preached. We are led to create spaces and practices that open our lives to God. Still, the decision is ours. Without such, we risk never entering into a deeper relationship with God.

God initiates the relationship, but we must take steps to respond and move toward God or the gift of relationship goes dormant on our end. As Wesley encouraged, sanctification (the process of being made whole or becoming holy) requires space for God.

Transformational spiritual leaders create space for God in their personal lives. If you don't have time or space for

God in your personal life, your public life will grow exceedingly empty.

If I were serving as pastor again, I would create more space for God in my personal life.

CHAPTER 8

Get a Plan

I would get a plan. According to Ram Charan in *Execution: The Discipline of Getting Things Done*, "Seventy percent of strategic failures are due to poor execution of leadership. It's rarely for lack of smarts or vision." Execution of strategy requires a plan. Without a plan, churches simply follow the calendar of what they did last year. Perhaps that is why people say, "That's what we have always done." Planning is that intentional process of where you are, what you are going to do and who you are going to reach. Goal setting is essential to accountability. It doesn't matter what system you use, just use a plan.

In the second chapter of the Gospel of John, Jesus' mother tells him their hosts have run out of wine. Perhaps she is urging him to do something about it, to turn the water into wine, or maybe she just wanted him to go to the market and buy some more wine. Who knows? I love Jesus' response, "It isn't my time." In other parts of the gospel, Jesus would respond to a question with, "It is the right time" (Jn. 12:23, paraphrase). In the garden on the night of his arrest, Jesus responded with, "It's time" (Jn. 17:1, paraphrase). It is obvious Jesus was working a plan. In fact, the Bible is fairly clear that God has been working a plan from the beginning of time. The life of Jesus was no accident; it was a part of God's unfolding plan.

If I were to be a local pastor again, I would get a plan and work that plan. If that plan didn't work I would stop, adjust the plan and begin to work *that* plan. If you don't put together a plan for your ministry in a particular church and mission field, your ministry will simply be guided by the calendar and the urgent needs of the day. Too many pastors simply flit from one trendy, shiny idea to the next; one day to the next, one Sunday to the next, one season to the next, year over year, without so much as a plan. If I were a pastor again, I would get a plan and work the plan.

Now don't just go off on your own plan. Each of us need to involve lay leaders from the community in creating the plan designed for the mission field. One of the first places to work with is your administrative board and your pastor parish relations team. Ask what does the mission field need? What is the impact to this church? What must happen? What could stop? What new ministry might we start? In my book, *10 Prescriptions for a Healthy Church* (Abingdon Press, 2015), there is a whole chapter on planning (Chapter 8: Strategic Ministry Planning).

It is hard to arrive somewhere if you don't set the destination from the outset. Without a destination, your GPS can only show you where you currently are; not where you are trying to go! What are your priorities during the next three to six months? What are three goals for this year? What are the small actions steps you could take and repeat over and over that would change the trajectory of this congregation?

If I were a pastor again, I would get a plan for the church and for my personal life and my professional life. Every church needs to know where it's going and every person, every pastor needs to know where they are headed personally and professionally. Otherwise, life just happens to you.

Some have said that ministry is a life of interruptions and that's true. However, that doesn't mean you can't have and work a plan. Plans can change! Every plan should start with Bible study and prayer. Every plan should start with learning about your mission field; the hurts of the people, the needs of the people. Listen to outside voices; be available, be intentional in learning. A good plan involves lots of people and takes some effort and time to figure out. Remember a plan is not the Ten Commandments written in stone. Plans are meant to be changed, adapted and changed some more. At best, plans are written in pencil. The mission of bringing people to Jesus Christ for the transformation of the world never changes, but plans on how to do that change on a regular basis.

No plan works unless you work it. Christians are pretty good at visioning the plan. When it comes to working the plan, the laborers are few and the harvest plentiful, as Jesus once said. We have been overly trained in strategy with little equipping in the area of execution. Sometimes, I have people have come up to me and said, "Your HCI plan didn't work!" My response? "It only works if *you* work it!" So, if I were a pastor again, I would get a plan and I would work the plan.

CHAPTER 9

Dig In

I would dig in. I would not simply arrive in my new mission field. I would live fully in the new space. In the book of Jeremiah, there is an ancient letter written from the prophet to the people of Israel who have recently been taken out of their homeland to live in a foreign land. They are distraught and uncertain of their future. Jeremiah is writing to them to encourage them. He doesn't tell them to fight in order to revolt and return home. Instead he tells them to continue to live their lives, to build houses, plant gardens, get married and have children and not to fight: "Seek the peace and prosperity of the city to which I have carried you into exile. Pray to the Lord for it, because if it prospers, you too will prosper" (Jer. 29:7). So, settle down, Jeremiah says, live in this new space and carve out a future that will one day be as meaningful as the old.

If I were to do it all over again, I would really move in to whatever community I was assigned to serve. I would settle down, even if I was unsure for how long I might be there. I would get to know my people. I would get to know what they want to do and what their lives are like. I find that many pastors struggle to truly move in, invest, and plant deep roots in a community. Some pastors are hesitant to put down roots for fear of hurting themselves or others when the time comes for them to leave. This is especially true of those in the United Methodist tradition who experience itineracy, our distinctive pattern of clergy deployment to the mission field.

My heart broke every time I left a church. I invested 125 percent of myself into Grace UMC, the church I helped to plant. When the time came to leave and become the senior pastor of a church three and a half hours to the east, it broke my heart to leave the people I had come to know and grown to love. When I arrived at my new appointment, I said to myself, "I'm not doing that again." I dug in again, only to find a whole new set of leaders and friends in ministry that I had not imagined.

I understand the temptation to avoid digging in and investing in a place and in people because it does hurt when you leave. Scripture gives us some guidance in this area of leadership. Jesus tells us that the shepherd enters the gate, "And the sheep listen to his voice. He calls his own sheep by name and leads them out. When he has brought out all his own, he goes on ahead of them, and his sheep follow him because they know his voice" (Jn. 10:3-4).

Leadership in the way of Jesus means getting to know your flock and allowing them to get to know you so that they recognize your voice and you learn to recognize theirs. You recognize the voice of the one you care about and invest in. A mother can recognize the sound of her child's cry in a crowded room. If we don't dig in and get to know the community where we have been placed, we lose the chance to live into the model that Jesus has set for us. Additionally, we hear John describe, and Eugene Petersen paraphrase in The Message, that the "Word became flesh and blood, and moved into the neighborhood" (Jn. 1:14).

To lead well, you have to move into the neighborhood.

You need to walk your dog with their dogs, shop where they shop, and live into the missional field. If you cannot physically live in the neighborhood of your church, you need to "live your neighborhood". I would encourage you to shop there, walk around there, eat with them in the community, go to kids' ballgames and sporting events, and ride your bike on the mission field's trails. Learn as much about the people as you can. My friend and clergy coach Jim Ozier calls this, "community exegesis." Where do you need to go to learn about the community, what meetings do you need to attend, what local places are the gathering space for the town or city?

This takes extra work and time but people know the difference. People recognize shepherds that live among them versus shepherds who are just biding their time until a better gig comes along.

I would dig in.

— CHAPTER 10 —

Listen Better

I would try to be a better listener. I have heard Jim Griffith say more than once that the hardest thing for pastors to do is to "strangle their teller." We are trained to think, to teach, to preach. I have yet to meet a pastor that took a listening course in seminary or college. Pastors often have to be intentional about listening and in order to be intentional, we have to resist talking.

As an extrovert myself, it requires a great deal of self-discipline for me not to speak. This includes not thinking about my response; concocting my reply to what you are saying. If I am thinking about my response, it means I have stopped listening to you. I need to go in here and keep my mouth shut.

James gives good advice that "Everyone should be quick to listen, slow to speak and slow to become angry" (1:19). However, pastors are rarely slow to speak. We often confuse our role to be the "answer person." This seems dangerous territory for a pastor to delve into. There will come a time when you have no answer and you and your people may experience an identity crisis – *your* identity crisis. You have to become comfortable saying, "I just don't know."

When I have had to make phone calls to people who have

lost a child, there are no words or answers to explain away that grief.

I have learned a lot from Senior Consultant of the G. Douglass Lewis Center for Church Leadership, Lovett Weems, about this. He says, Leaders do not need answers. Leaders must have the right questions. Really, it's about asking questions, and asking better questions. I find that as I go into a conversation or meeting, I need to do way more listening than talking.

My natural tendency is to do all the talking. Being intentional, I would devise a set of questions for any conversation. Eventually, this can become quite natural so that even for coffee conversations you can have a bank of questions in your head to offer during a session. Developing a set of questions allows me to trick my brain into thinking that I am actually talking! The questions allow the group space to talk. I am learning from listening to their responses in order to ask better questions.

This is not any truer than in a death in the congregation. When someone dies, as a pastor, I sit down with a set of questions and just listen and write. There has been no better experience for learning the technique of good listening than in these pastoral moments.

In order to be authentic in walking alongside people in their grief, you must listen. This skill can be applied beyond those moments of pastoral care into the contentious committee meeting, or the uncomfortable marital counseling session or a difficult staff conversation.

Another key skill to develop in listening is understanding the value of silence. I have not always valued silence. It made me uncomfortable. I saw silence as the enemy. I would try to fill the empty spaces of conversations. However, I have come to value silence in a conversation. I have discovered that silence speaks loudly and that we must let silence speak for itself.

My experience working in local churches through the Healthy Church Initiative was great for developing this skill. I would occasionally watch my colleagues try to rescue someone from an awkward silence. We all too often jump in to fill the gap. There is nothing like a pregnant pause to understand someone or a situation better.

The same is true within a sermon. A pause. A bit of silence allows the people listening and the preacher to take a moment, to settle in and to truly hear the Word of God speak into the life of the community. Listening makes you ask questions of your people, your mission field and of scripture.

Ultimately, good preaching is about asking good questions – of the text and of God. Don't be in a big hurry to answer it. Life isn't meant to be solved. It's meant to be lived and that includes the hard parts of living. You don't have to explain it. We do give it meaning; we help understand the situation in light of the faithful life, but we can't fix it or explain it away.

If you cannot figure out how to deeply listen to the people you can see, how in the world are you going to listen to the unseen God? God comes in the small, still voice, the gentle whisper and in the sheer silence (1 Kgs. 19:12). If this is true, I am going to miss a lot of what God has to say. It has been my experience that God rarely speaks over the sound of my own voice.

I still mess this up 90 percent of the time. I continue to talk more than needed, but am coming to realize how critical this skill is to good pastoral leadership. These days, I am a better listener. I wish I had been one earlier in my ministry. I wonder what I have missed.

I would be a better listener.

CHAPTER 11

Take Time for Family

I would take time for my family. Ministers can often find themselves suffering from the "I am indispensable" syndrome. There are three problems with this:

(1) Mistaking yourself as *the* plan rather than simply part *of* the plan. In our roles as pastors, especially in ministry models that are pastor-centric, we can get confused and think we are the plan rather than part of the plan. In your neck of the woods, you might be tempted to think that you are absolutely necessary to God's ministry on earth. You have been appointed to this work; God has called you, therefore, without you, the ministry cannot happen. You might tell that lie to motivate yourself, but it is a lie. Part of becoming fully human, which is what Jesus displays for us in his lifetime ministry, is in realizing that you are replaceable. You are not indispensable. I am not indispensable. Everyone, and I mean, everybody, is replaceable. This isn't a bad thing. It is something we should celebrate because it is the lived promise of God. The Israelites probably thought Moses was the only person who could lead them into the Promised Land. It wasn't so, however. God values purpose over personality.

If you take regular time away from the church to renew yourself, further educate yourself, or just simply be with God apart from others (Lk. 5:16), you will discover that upon

return, the church is still there. There is always plenty to
be done. Much of what we do can wait a week or two for you
to take a break. One of our Missouri pastors, Jim Downing,
was on a trip to Israel when the historic downtown church
building that is part of his ministry caught fire. Jim could
have spent time beating himself up; if he had not gone away,
he would have been there for the community. Instead, while
he was on that long flight back, the church community cared
for one another, the associate pastor stepped up and into the
congregational care role. Even if Jim had been home, the
church would still have burned down. There wasn't anything
he could have done. Jim is a part of God's plan, but Jim isn't
God's plan.

(2) The second problem with indispensable syndrome
is that it means I am trying to bring in the kingdom by my
own efforts. I have witnessed this temptation in myself and
in other pastors, thinking that we have the ability to "save"
something or someone. This Savior complex can lead to
overwork and burnout. I have seen some cases where pastors
have worked themselves into early retirement or medical
leave, or in some cases, an early death. In small churches,
the idea that the church cannot function without you can
become intoxicating.

It can be a real ego-boost. It can also mean that an
unhealthy co-dependency has developed. You might think
that the church can't function without you, but the reality
is that you cannot function without the church. You have to
develop mental, emotional and spiritual strength to prevent
your ego from entering into this kind of imbalance. You are
not the Savior. I am not the Savior. The Church is not the
savior. It is not. The Savior is Jesus Christ. The Church is the
instrument Christ uses to the offer hope to the world. Jesus
is our salvation. As a disciple of Jesus Christ, you partici-

pate with the spirit for that purpose. Paul described it this way, "I planted the seed, Apollos watered it, but God has been making it grow" (1 Cor. 3:6).

Now, hardworking folks can grow things on their own blood, sweat and tears for some time. You know what I have discovered in my ministry in those cases? When you leave, it goes up in smoke. Working harder is not always working smarter. And, it is sometimes working against God rather than in cooperation with God.

(3) And, finally, and perhaps most importantly, thinking yourself indispensable often means that you are neglecting some of the most important relationships entrusted to you. If I had it to do over again, I would disciple my family more. I took my kids to church all the time. What I didn't do was introduce them to Jesus. My son Joe says he got enough church in the first 16 years of his life to last him a lifetime! What I hear in Joe's statement is that I mistakenly taught him that loving Jesus meant hanging out in a church building all the time, not having a life outside the walls of the church. I failed Joe on that count.

So, I would take more time for family outside of the church and outside of my paid work. I never tucked my two children Joe and Amy into bed. My wife Susan got that honor. I was out in the community every evening, at a church meeting or Bible study. However, if there is a gift to clergy, it is the gift of flexibility. It is about how you use the time. You cannot see it through the same lens as other professions. So, I did wake up my kids every morning as Susan got ready and left for her teaching position. I made them breakfast and put them on the school bus. I also picked them up after school and spent their first hour at home with them. Still, immediately after dinner, my church work began and I was back at it.

When I am with family, I try hard to be fully present with the family. I have to work on this all the time. As a pastor, we talked too much church at home. Every night at dinner, we talked a lot about church, the building project, the next mission team launch, the growth plan, the new discipleship plan. I would try to cultivate life outside church with family. Make a standing date with your significant other or a close friend. Schedule time on your calendar and protect it with the people important in your life. Incorporate your life into their interests so they know how important they are to you. Part of being a healthy, self-differentiated leader is knowing when you are carrying someone's grief, the argument from the trustees meeting, or the strain of financial hardship into your marriage bed, your family dinner and your friendships suffer.

I would take time for my family.

— CHAPTER 12 —

Get On the Team

I would get on the team or get off the team. I am keen on pastors being sold out on their local church. It is the hope of the world. The gathered community of God is the primary place where people are formed and made into the image of Christ. This is the best way for us to experience God. This is the vehicle that God chose to change the world. If you are not sold out on this idea, then what in the world are you doing?

I say the same for whatever denomination, association or affiliation of which you are currently a part. I don't understand pastors who complain about the denomination or their church. I am enthusiastic about being United Methodist. It is the way in which I have come to know Christ. I happen to think the Wesleyan way of salvation is the best way for contemporary Christians to understand their relationship with God and others. That is what drives me to share the Good News with others. If you are so unhappy with the denomination, why are you here? That doesn't mean you cannot reform or call to change. My entire ministry has been a call to change from within, but ask yourself, why are you calling or changing? Is it out of a deep love or criticism only? Don't claim the privileges of the denomination without claiming the responsibilities of the organization. Team members earn the right to help make change from within. If you're only interested in Monday morning quarterbacking, go play somewhere else.

Early on in my ministry, I had to stop participating in clergy covenant groups. I understand that there are many healthy covenant groups and I hear a lot of our clergy have powerful covenant groups formed in the Wesleyan tradition of bands. Still, the groups I used to see form among clergy were not the same. It was a coffee clutch filled with gossip and complaints wrapped in a faux spirituality. Jesus said, "Where two or three gather in my name, there am I with them" (Matt. 18:20). I say, where two or three are gathered, you better hope the spirit of God is there. Now, everybody needs their place to vent and pastors should identify safe places for that purpose. Healthy colleagues allow you to vent, but they don't let you stay in that place week after week and month after month.

I have been tempted twice in ministry to leave my team. Once early on, I was offered a job as a fire chief in Colorado. It paid more money and seemed to have much less of a head-ache than some of my current "flustrations." For the first time in my life, I thought, "maybe." A second time happened after what I call "the big melt-down" in a church meeting at the new church at Grace. At about age 36, I walked into the office of my District Superintendent, with all my credentialed paperwork, my ordination papers and license and threw them down on his desk. I said, "I'm done! I'm not doing this anymore!" He just looked at me as I headed towards the door. As I was on my way out, another District Superintendent who overhead my commotion, said, "If you can drive away without looking back, you better drive. If you have to look back, you might want to slow down before you make that decision." I have never forgotten that bit of advice. We can all get to that place. For some of us more hotheaded ones, we may have a tendency to make rash decisions. Healthy colleagues and trusted conversation partners can make sure you have really thought through your decisions. I cooled off eventually and got my paperwork back.

There will always be what I call, "flustration," the state of agitated frustration. "Flustration" is a real thing. There is no organization where "flustration" does not exist. All pastors are going to experience this almost-career ending "flustration" in their ministry. This is hard stuff. People are challenging to work with and obstacles are always around every corner. There will be days where you think, surely there is something else I could be doing with my life or my time. I would guess that if you don't have that moment once or twice in an entire 40-year career, then you probably aren't doing it right. You haven't invested enough. You are operating only at the surface. You get "flustrated" because you care.

Why be lukewarm? The church of Laodicea got a stern reprimand for being neither too hot nor too cold (Rev. 3:16). Jesus seemed to have one or two of these moments in the course of his ministry. Jesus said to Peter, "Get behind me, Satan! You are a stumbling block to me" (Matt. 16:23). This was probably not the most pastoral moment in his career. He also cursed a fig tree (Mk. 11:12-14). Jesus got "flustrated." If you're not invested, it's hard to imagine getting this upset. Don't let that overwhelm you or the team. If you don't like the team you are playing for, get yourself another team. Decide whose team you are on, get on that team and be a good and loyal teammate.

I am intensively passionate for being United Methodist, as long as it is in service to my loyalty to Jesus Christ. At the end of the day, if you cannot be enthusiastically Wesleyan or United Methodist, perhaps you ought not be the pastor. Don't be wishy-washy or lukewarm. I am happy for someone to be United Methodist. I fly the United Methodist flag, but that doesn't mean I don't try to bring change to my tribe. That goes for members outside my own tribe. If you are a Baptist or Lutheran, be the best Baptist or Lutheran you can be for your team. Be sold out on your local church. That's your team. The gathered people of God are where people are primarily and formally made into disciples. You either believe that or you don't. If you don't like that work and don't care for the people involved in that work, get out.

I get sick of pastor colleagues who whine and complain all the time. Who wants to hang out with people who are miserable all the time? Your congregation sees right through that. They know the difference between someone who is sold out for their local church and those who are just bidding their time until the next thing. Life is too short. Quit already.

I would get on the team or get off the team.

CHAPTER 13

Get Out of the Building

I would get out of the building and hang out with my people. Hanging out with your people is how you do pastoral care. A tragedy is the one moment in which you get to peer into people's lives in ways that other people don't. That is a moment in their life and yours that you don't ever get back. Being with people in times of crisis is important but congregational care includes hanging out with them when there isn't a crisis to be found. Part of digging in is discovering the hang-out places unique to your community and getting involved in activities outside the church.

Upon moving into the community in Celeste, Texas during my student appointment, the superintendent of schools happened to be United Methodist and shared with me a tradition in that community. The school had three buses and three bus routes, three churches and three pastors. He said it had been their tradition that each of the pastors would drive one of the three bus routes throughout the school year. Looking back, I'm fairly convinced he made this up. However, the Baptist minister did drive one of the routes. (The previous United Methodist pastor refused.) The superintendent stated that the school needed a bus driver. I said yes because, quite honestly, as a seminary student and young husband, I needed the money. The $400 per month I was paid to drive the bus came close to meeting my bill from seminary, which was $405 (my apologies to current students). Susan and I didn't have any credit history and had no student loans. God provided through the school superintendent and the school bus gig worked out to pay for my seminary.

I drove for two years, grateful for that $400/month. Another thing this opportunity provided was in learning my community. I picked kids up from all three churches and the surrounding communities. Driving the school bus allowed me access not only into the lives of the children, but into those of the parents as well. I earned their respect and the privilege of entering into their lives because I carried special cargo. I also earned a reputation as the "fast bus driver." I had to get that bus into the barn in the morning with enough time to go home, shower and get to class in Dallas. Then, when I'd get back in the afternoon, I had to drive the bus, get home and to the church for ministry. The kids loved it; the parents, not so much.

When I was in Celeste, our youth group went from three or four kids to 25. Why? Because I met them on the bus. When I arrived in Celeste, people would tell me the reason the church didn't have children's ministry because there weren't any kids. Yet, there had to be. I find that state governments do not build schools where there are no children. Right in their backyard was a school system loaded with children.

Susan and I had a great time getting to know the children of that community. Between that and joining the local fire department as a volunteer, I knew everyone and everyone knew me within weeks of my arrival.

I would get out of the building.

— CHAPTER 14 —

Read a Lot

I would read; a lot. One of the first bits of advice
Harold Dodds gave me was to read, read and read some more.
He believed that one should read a sermon from someone
else once a week.

A few months after graduating seminary, Dodds asked
me, "What are you reading?" I promptly replied, "If I had my
druthers, nothing ever again." School did not come easy for
me. It's a miracle I finished graduate school. Now, I recognize my academic and reading challenges as an undiagnosed
learning disability. However, it seems that as a Methodist
preacher, I wouldn't get off so easy. Learning through reading would be an ever present part of my ministry. Dodds
told me you had to be reading – a book every week, a sermon
from someone else every week.

He was right. Not every great reader is a great preacher,
but every great preacher is a great reader. The more you
read, the better preacher and teacher you become. The more
diversified a reader you can be, the better preacher you will
become. We are people of the book and no one took that
more seriously than John Wesley. Wesley read voraciously
throughout his ministry and was diverse in his selections
from theology to science to medicine. John Wesley's writing
to preacher John Premboth on August 17, 1760 said:

"What has exceedingly hurt you in time past, nay, and I fear to this day, is want of reading. I scarce ever knew a preacher read so little. And perhaps, by neglecting it, you have lost the taste for it. Hence your talent in preaching does not increase. It is just the same as it was seven years ago. It is lively, but not deep; there is little variety, there is no compass of thought. Reading only can supply this, with meditation and daily prayer. You wrong yourself greatly by omitting this. You can never be a deep preacher without it, any more than a thorough Christian.[8]

Another thing I have learned about reading is that you can develop heroes you never meet in person. When you read about one of the first Methodist bishops in America, Francis Asbury, or Henry Foxall, a dedicated Methodist layman, you can meet a hero within the pages of a good book. A lot of the people I admire and imitate are people I have never met. I have every book the early 20th century pastor Henry Fosdick has ever written. I came across a book of sermons of Fosdick's when visiting a used book store in downtown Kansas City with Harold Dodds. To this day, I think they are some of the finest written sermons I have come across. I continue to draw on his books of sermons and prayers for inspiration to this day.

In order to be a preacher who reads, you need to set aside time specifically for that purpose. In some ways, your congregation is paying for you to study and continue to learn on their behalf. I read the paper every morning. Today, I read it on my phone, but it is important to know what is going on in the world. In today's world, watching and listening are nice compliments to reading. Podcasts and audiobooks allow you to read books in the midst of travel and exercise.

8 Quoted in Ben Witherington's *Is There a Doctor in the House?: An Insider's Story and Advice on Becoming a Bible Scholar,* pg. 71.

My wife and I try to incorporate watching documentaries into our continued learning plan. In my ministry, this was one of the most crucial choices and decisions I ever made, even though it was not a natural choice. Thankfully, a wiser colleague started me on a path toward learning through reading.

I would read; a lot.

— CHAPTER 15 —

Tell the People About Jesus

I would tell people about Jesus. One of my great fears in ministry is that we have taught people to fall in love with our churches rather than to fall in love with Jesus. We have given church to the next generation and it has left them wanting. I don't want to slight the organized church. It's not that it is bad. And, membership is not the worst thing in the world. But, it seems that many churches confused their purpose in making members of an organization rather than introducing people to Jesus and making disciples. Members are not synonymous with disciples.

People are disinterested in just church, but highly interested in spiritual things that can and will lead them into a faith community. If it's only about the organized church, when that church changes – the worship times change, the style of music shifts or the building falls down, some people cannot fathom connecting to another one. We have failed those people. "Our hope is built on nothing less than Jesus Christ's blood and righteousness," as the song goes. It is not built within four walls and locked into the pews. People need to fall in love with Jesus, not the church building or even the organization; so when they go out to share Jesus with others, they are connecting them directly to Christ and in doing so, sharing the community of believers.

It is all about relationships: Who are they? Where are they in their life? In the book, *Get Their Name*, my co-authors and I name those opportunities as "crossover moments." These moments are often about a commonality you experience; an article of clothing, a name, an experience, a hobby; anything you might use to identify a common connection with another person. This allows you to continue the conversation. Relationships always trump doctrine. People want to know you. They want to be sure they can trust you.

Through relationships built on trust and respect, you can begin to ask, "Where is God in this? Does your faith have anything to do with this? What might God say about this?" There is no science behind making the transition from, "How is your day going" to "How is it with your soul?" I think a key question to introducing Christ into the conversation is asking, "Where are you?" This question is one that all people think about even though they may not articulate it that way. Where are you in your life? Everyone is always assessing this. It's a deeply human question. We all – including the non-religious among us – need to wrestle with this question – "What am I doing? Where am I?"

Rarely do I have these questions with someone I do not know. My first coffee with you will just be about relationships. Build relationships first and then bring up Jesus. Help them create a relationship with Jesus first, and the church, second.

I would tell people about Jesus.

— CHAPTER 16 —

Disciple Someone

I would disciple someone. Actually, I would always be discipling someone and teaching others how to disciple. If I have a regret in my life as a pastor, it is that I think I gave people more church than I gave them Christ. I would want a "do over" so that the people I pastored walked away feeling like I gave them Christ; not my opinions, not great big theological terminology, but Christ.

John Wesley's effort to serve Jesus Christ by preaching him is probably second to none. He once wrote after visiting a town to preach, "I gave them Christ."

When you're preaching, instead of giving your opinions or the latest psychology, make sure you talk about Jesus. I have heard a lot of sermons that left me wondering, "Where was Jesus in all that?" Even in my own ministry, I could have asked that question at times.

In every church I ever served, the membership class consisted of primarily three classes. In the first class, I gave them United Methodist history, polity and doctrine. In the second class, I gave them information about our specific local church and the "great things we do."

At the third class, I introduced the staff who went about the work of saying "all the great things we do" then asked,

"Which one of these things would you like to do?" At the end
of this last class, we talked about the membership vows. If
I were doing it today, I might talk about United Methodist
history and polity at some point in the class, but I would first
ask folks to, "Tell me about your faith." "When was the last
time you experienced God?" "Let me tell you about the five
ways this church can help you ask better questions and grow
your spiritual life." I would not give them the list of things
they could come do for the church.

My biggest regret is that I did it that way. I didn't realize I was giving them the Church instead of Jesus. I didn't
know to do it. I didn't realize what we are doing wrong.
We were selling the church. We were giving reasons why it
would be better if they came to our church rather than the
church down the street. We have a better...worship service...
choir...community outreach...Sunday School...youth group;
we were selling the church, and saw other churches as our
competition.

We would hand those interested in membership a card to
select in what part of this church they would like to participate, thinking that this would connect them to the church.
Then, we would wonder why after six months, they stopped
coming.

The dropout rate for our new members stood around 50
percent. When we questioned this, we wondered what was
wrong with them? Why wouldn't they want to be a part of a
great church? We wondered if maybe we didn't get enough
commitment from them; or, maybe we didn't get them
plugged into the right part of the church. What we didn't
realize was that we were plugging them into the wrong thing.

The truth is, we gave them the church rather than Jesus.
It was about membership and once new people joined the

church, we felt we were done. If I had a do-over, I would give them Jesus. I would ask them to tell me their story. Our classes would focus around discipleship, how to grow their faith and not about the church. I would talk about spiritual life and growth. I would talk about discipleship. I would talk about the things they need to do to have a vibrant, spiritual life. I would plug them into Jesus instead of trying to plug them into church.

What are the practices you are teaching people to experience a more vibrant spiritual life? When it is all over I want people to say, I gave them Christ. I didn't offer opinions, great big words; I gave them Christ. Offering Christ begins the disciple's journey. Teaching people to fall in love with a local church causes heartbreak when the church is called to do a new thing.

People resist new styles of worship and new ways of doing ministry if their focus is on the church rather than Christ. Instead, falling in love with Christ allows your connection to the community to evolve over time. It allows your relationship to Christ and the community to deepen and helps you see the mission despite your personal preferences. One of the primary questions we ask of our pastors today is "Who are you discipling?" If you aren't discipling someone, how can you expect them to disciple someone else?

I would disciple somebody.

— CHAPTER 17 —

Have Fun

I would have some fun along the way. If you're not having any fun, you're probably in the wrong place. American physician Richard Clarke Cabot developed a theory about true healthiness (What Men Live by: Work, Play, Love, Worship by Richard Clarke Cabot)9. He said life is like a cross. One arm of the cross stood for work, another for worship, the third for rest and play. The fourth arm was love. His years of experience in cardiology showed that when this cross moved out of balance, when one arm of the cross overwhelmed the others, life became unhealthy.

While I think there is truth in Dr. Cabot's analogy, I think that "balance" can be an overused word. There were times in my life when I may have been out of balance in any one of these areas. It is my belief, though, that had I been in balance, I wouldn't have gotten things done.

You don't live a balanced life and plant new churches. Balance is seasonal. It is important to recognize those seasons of unbalance and understand that they cannot continue forever. I sometimes find that those who live a full life of balance, do not accomplish much.

There is an old saying, "All work and no play makes Jack

9 Richard C. Cabot, *What Men Live by: Work, Play, Love, Worship.* Palala Press (2015).

a dull boy." I would amend that proverb to, "All work and no play makes Bob a dull man." No one says, "I want to have some fun today! I'm going to call the preacher!" Most people wouldn't dare think of calling their pastors to go hunting, play golf or go to the races. It is more likely that a person might think of their ministers as dull rather than exciting. However, I think having a good time is important and I'm committed to having a good time.

I'm going to enjoy what I'm doing and I've never had a church where I didn't have a good time. No matter what I'm doing, I'm going to have some fun along the way. Even at my first Annual Conference as a presiding bishop, I said we were going to have some fun, and we did!

I would make sure there was fun along the way. I've never seen a growing church that wasn't having fun. The other side of this is that churches who aren't having fun, are rarely growing. People need enjoyment. They need fun. You can tell those churches who are having a good time by what they hang on the wall, how they interact with each other; the atmosphere is happy and light. They like being together, worshiping together, serving together and they like having fun together.

One church I pastored sponsored several "fun" groups. We had a Chief's Club that attended football games together. There was a men's group that took a fishing trip to Canada. We had a softball team. And, there was a Plus 50 group that took a bus trip every summer. They all had fun.

Beyond the local church work, pastors need to discover fun in their personal lives. Find something that makes you happy, gives you purpose and allows you to connect with God and others more deeply. For me the fun was the fire department. In practically every community I have served, I volunteered at the fire department. It was a great opportunity for me to spend time outside the church serving and not thinking about the church budget or the list of maintenance projects from the trustees. It also provided me with space to hang out with men – many of whom were not churched – and to remember what life is like for those outside the church walls. Yes, this was an opportunity for me to get their name and to share Jesus with them. I have written about that in other places, but really, helping serve the community through fire protection and fire safety education was a passion for me.

What is your playground? Is it board games, sports, hiking, sewing, cosplay, music, yoga, travel? Own it and do it. Go have some fun.

I would have fun.

— CHAPTER 18 —

Celebrate Wins

Looking back on several decades of ministry provides you with a list of "I wish I hads." One area of ministry leadership I was not great about was stopping and celebrating wins. I was always ready to move on to the next thing. Creating intentional times celebrating people's ministries and their own commitments is an important part of spiritual leadership; not because it's part of the vision, but it's fun! People want to be a part of a winning team. Consider all the people who jumped on the Kansas City Royals bandwagon in 2015 when they headed to the World Series. I say, "the more the merrier."

Discover ways in your local church that you can celebrate even the tiniest win to help people feel good about the hard work of discipleship. Even Jesus stopped to enjoy life and celebrate (Jn. 2:1-12). I think he even told a joke or two (Mk. 10:25). Human beings were made for celebrations and fun. That's why Christmas is such a big hit in churches among the faithfully committed and the spontaneous worshipers. People love celebrating!

I sometimes hear pastors lament that they haven't had a win in years. Perhaps we set our sights on too big a prize. You have to win a lot of ballgames before you get to go to the World Series. Before that, you have to win a lot of batting practices, a lot of fieldwork and a lot of gym workouts. In one of the small churches I served, a small group of women faithfully combed the local newspapers and school districts newsletters to cut out clippings and add a note of congratulations to members of the community. It was one of the ways they loved their church community. It was also one of the ways they celebrated others and had fun.

People crave fun and celebration. Help young people create the scrapbooks of mementos and encouragement from their school years. Show them that there is a group of people rooting them on beyond their circle of immediate family and friends. Build a community around them.

You have to get some little wins before you can get the big ones. We do it with children all the time. Potty training is a lesson on celebrating the little wins. Achievement charts littered with stars document little successes in school. How many homemade chore charts with "be kind," "no whining" and "clean up your room" have you made or seen? The church ought to be as affirming.

The work of discipleship is hard. People who are growing in their faith need encouragement. They need affirmation of the way the Spirit is working in their lives. People get enough negative in their life and the Church has a reputation of offering nothing but judgment. We have an opportunity to name and affirm the work of the Holy Spirit in their lives. Set aside time each week to write out three note cards to people in your community and beyond naming the ways you see God working in their lives.

It was late in my career that I figured this out when we started celebrating our volunteers and their gifts. We looked for any way we could affirm people. We would commission new leaders, pray over and celebrate Sunday School leaders, send off mission teams at the airport with a crowd and celebrate them upon their return. It gets more challenging to do the bigger the church but those ways of celebrating community can happen even in the smallest circle. This is one of the reasons why it is so hard to get rid of "Joys and Concerns" in small church culture.

For many of the people in your community, this is their one opportunity each week to affirm one another and to feel heard. If you are going to move away from this part of the informal liturgy of the church, you need to discover other ways of affirming people and naming the joys and concerns. We often remove this from worship as we grow, but don't provide other outlets for this expression and wonder why the congregation is upset.

CHAPTER 19

What's Your Point?

I would get to the point in my sermons. By that I mean I would spend more time on sermon delivery and less time on content. I don't mean that content is not important; it very much is. Instead, what I discovered through years of sermon preparation is that how we say something is just as important, if not more so, than what we say.

This has been a long lesson in leadership for me. In my early days, I was very worried about saying the right things. I see this in a lot of inexperienced and insecure preachers. They want to say all the right things as if there is some magic formula of words in sequence that will convert and convict people. Perhaps there is and I never discovered it. What I did discover was that people respond to a simple, passionate message. They respond in belief, or at least exploration, when they think that you believe something.

So, if I had to do it all over again, I would arrive at a simple, salient point sooner in my preparation and spend all the rest of my time honing that message through delivery. Powerful communication is more than the words we use. Delivery, cadence, eye contact, speed, humor and slang are all just as important as the message you deliver. How does my voice sound? What nonverbal cues do I want to compliment my delivery? How might I use the preaching space to better drive home my point? What illustrations help make this a relevant subject in the lives of my audience? In what ways can technology – visual and audio effects – affirm my message? Most preachers spend 95 percent of their time on content and five percent on delivery. We might be wise to switch that up. Twentieth century media theorist Marshall McLuhan coined the phrase, "The medium is the message."10 What he meant by this was that people tend to focus on the obvious, which is the content. However, in the process, we largely miss the structural changes that are introduced to us subtly, or over long periods of time through the medium. Now, he used "medium" in a very broad sense. One of the ways he described it was through the illustration of a light bulb.

While a light bulb does not have content in the way that a newspaper has stories or a TV has programs, it is a medium that has a social effect. A light bulb enables people to create spaces during nighttime that would otherwise be enveloped by darkness.

McLuhan describes the light bulb as a medium without any content. For churches, the pastor and even the worship itself is the medium. The entire experience, including the delivery of the sermon, has a social effect on the congregation over time. This is even more apparent in a world filled with changing social technology. How churches deliver ways of getting to know Jesus – through small groups, one-on-one apprenticeship, live-streaming worship or group text prayer chains – all of the multiple ways of communicating are an essential part of the message itself.

In one church I visited, the pastor (a musician) spent several minutes introducing the opening song for an Advent

---

[10] Marshall McLuhan, *Understanding Media* McGraw-Hill (1964)

service. The song was difficult to sing and the congregation never got comfortable with it. Because it was so difficult, I guarantee that by the end of the first verse no one remembered why we were singing it. It's like that with sermons. If you spend all your time on content and no time on delivery, people aren't going to remember the content.

This is not to say that content is not important. I visited a church once to hear a young person and happened to sit next to a woman who had heard me preach early on in my career. As this young man preached, the woman leaned over to me and said, "He preaches a lot like you did when you were his age. But, you had something to say." The young man had bucket loads of enthusiasm, but no content. Sunday after Sunday after Sunday that won't work. People see through it. Though he had the enthusiasm for the work, he didn't have anything in his bucket. Really good content without delivery won't work either.

I have learned my best sermon delivery techniques from standup comedians. I used to go to the comedy club in Kansas City in Westport, not because I particularly liked their content, but to learn from their delivery approach. They knew how to "hang a word," meaning, they knew how to pause for dramatic affect. They use a word, pause and let it set there for a time to let space form around it. Sometimes, the message I receive from presentations arrives more from delivery than the content.

In one recent presentation, I was particularly intrigued by the turns of phrases the presenter used to transition to different topics: "down shift," "double-clutch," "skip gears." All of these turns of phrase were used to trigger the listener's memory. In other words, "I'm about to make a point here..." The phrases were unrelated to the topic, but they caused the listeners to remember what was said and what was coming up next. That's what comics do. Their delivery causes us to remember what they said.

I would get to the point in my sermons.

— CHAPTER 20 —

Do Not Hate

I would try not to hate. This might seem counter to the identity of a pastor and it is, but every pastor I've ever met is human. Human beings have the capacity to hate. And, let's face it, hating is fun. A lot of my colleagues might dismiss the notion of hate as unlikely within their own souls or the pastors they know. Jealousy, revenge, aggravation, resentfulness, bitterness and annoyance are all variations on hate.

Turning my imagination loose thinking of all the diabolic ways I could get even with somebody, someone who has wronged me, hurt me or humbled me can become a fantasy. A fantasy that one can return to over and over. A fantasy that can build into a plan. Such plans feed on malice and in extreme cases, if gone too far, can end in self-destruction and even murder.   Preachers are prime suspects for becoming haters because we continually run into frustrations. Our identities are bound up in our work. We need somebody to take the blame.

I'd try not to get angry as much if I were back in the local church. As a young pastor, I did not always have complete control of my emotions. I could run a little hot. I could be quick to anger. The thing I struggled with most is that it is so easy to get angry with people in your congregation. And, I don't have a sufficient answer to why that is. I look back and there were people at whom I expressed anger and I wish I had not.

Consider this, as a pastor, have you ever had the thought, "If only they were not a part of my church, everything would all go smoothly." My experience has been that if you have reached the point of thinking that way, you may actually succeed in removing them from your church. That's not our job, though, is it? Our job is to tend to the sheep that have been placed in our care. There will always be a sheep that gets lost or wanders off constantly or bleats and bleats and bleats. Jesus seemed to think those sheep were important, too. The truth is, there will always someone in your church who is going to frustrate you, challenge you and disappoint you.

If I knew then what I know now, I would try to grow my emotional intelligence and learn to better control my emotions.

In leadership development, we know that your IQ is important, but your EQ (emotional intelligence) might be even more so. Perhaps it is a part of aging that we gain better control over our emotions, we are better at recognizing them, sharing how we feel through our words and managing our emotions in certain settings. That has not always been the case with me.

In one church, we started a preschool. The endeavor was not going well and we were losing money. We had just moved into a new building and we didn't have any margin to lose money. There was anxiety about the drain on our ministry and our ability to manage the budget. After some debate, we decided we had to be done with the preschool. We shut it down; effective immediately. We sent notices out on Friday that there would be no school on Monday. As you might imagine, that action did not go over well and several folks got angry. Preschool families were so upset that a group of women showed up to protest on Sunday morning after worship carrying their babies. Unbeknownst to me, they had called the local newspaper who had also arrived on site. The women complained that the church had shut the school down without their permission. From my position in the sanctuary, I could see these people gathering in the lobby. They were causing a commotion and handing out fliers to every person leaving the church.

I walked down the aisle and asked them as nicely as possible to please stop in light of Sunday morning worship. I asked that they not disrupt folks in between services. This was my first encounter with any kind of protest. I will never forget how angry I got because their complaints were messing up my Sunday morning. I even had a lay person call the police to exit people. As one lady was leaving the building, she yelled at me as I opened the door. I honestly don't remember what I said to her in that moment. Unfortunately, what I got quoted in the newspaper as saying was, "And don't let the door hit you in the *** on the way out!" Too this day, I can feel the heat in my face with the recollection of this event. I was so angry. Their actions may or may not have been warranted or appropriate, but my actions certainly were not either. My anger did not help the situation. It never does. I look back and think, "What was I thinking?!" It took a long time to live it down and to repair my reputation with others.

It's good to remember that if you become angry and reactive, and words leave your mouth, you can't get them back. You can apologize, but the hurt is already done and you can't undo it. Our culture is not very good with dealing with big emotions like fear, sadness and anger. We don't know how to disagree without it escalating into a full-on fight. Our niceness culture sometimes doesn't give us permission to state our true feelings. As I have gotten older, I think it's fine and important to state your position, share your disagreement, to even name the emotions you are feeling. However, to do that well, you must have processed those emotions outside of the situation – with God through prayer, a good friend, a trusted circle or a professional. Getting angry doesn't help.

If I were to do it all over again, I would also understand that if you're in the ministry, you are in the public sphere. Always. Your identity as a pastor never disappears. You are never off the clock. You can't get publicly angry with people. You don't get do overs. Even if you apologize and do all the right things; you don't get it back. The good opinion of you among others can be eroded in a moment. This is even more of an issue today than ever before for pastors. We live in a world that is constantly being documented. Bad behavior is filmed by strangers and uploaded to the Internet in minutes. Most of a pastor's Sunday morning experience is being live streamed or recorded for playback at a later time. Social media networks share content at a speed so quickly that we refer to it as "going viral." Within the office in which I work, bad behavior on social media is becoming more and more of an issue. Pastors have been exited out of licensed ministry because of inappropriate posts on social media. The reasons are as diverse as there are people but the common denominator between most of the cases is that the person did not appropriately deal with the emotions they were experiencing. There was a gap in their emotional intelligence that got illuminated on social media.

I would try not to hate.

CHAPTER 21

Know What You Believe

I would know what I believed and be as consistent as possible with that message. Consistency is not the same thing as repetition but it does include a return to a singular message or action or commitment so that people understand. I don't want to listen to a preacher who doesn't know what he/she believes. Spotty or unpredictable theology is not helpful for a congregation. Spotty theology includes inconsistent preaching.

If you are a preacher that latches on to every new thing that comes along, it is no wonder that lay people don't know what to believe. The latest fad is always a temptation for preachers. We have all experienced pastors who pick up on all the new ideas and new concepts, even if they contradict the past Sunday's sermon or the mission of the church. This is especially true with mission work.

Many pastors apply the "let's throw a bunch of things against the wall and see what sticks" theory to missional engagement, rather than try to create relationships built on equity and trust through a deep commitment. These churches tend to be churches with missions instead of missional churches.

I've heard people say of their pastor, "She's never met a

special offering she didn't love" or "This is his latest project of the month." Generosity in our financial and time resources is great, but our missional approach, as well as our theological approach to proclamation should be consistent and embedded in a deeply held belief.

Be consistent and know what you believe. This is easier said than done. Know what your church is consistently going to offer. Know what a person's next step will be. Many churches operate on a "we will see what the day brings" mentality. I think we are called to be more intentional and thoughtful than that.

For ordained elders in the United Methodist tradition, we are called to "order" the church. We are called to organize it in such a way that disciples of Christ are made. This requires a consistent and intentional approach in belief and practice.

Jesus was consistent. He was consistent in his proclamation which is why three of our four Gospels have many of the same teachings. One of his consistent themes was the idea that God was a father with outstretched arms welcoming the child home. It didn't matter where the child had been or what the child had done, the father was always expectant and ready to receive the child into his arms.

The second consistent theme of Jesus' preaching was to provide outstretched arms to those who were hurting or marginalized, to lift somebody who was down and out or to hold somebody who was broken. Jesus had a theology of outstretched arms. He preached on it consistently during his Galilean ministry. I imagine he repeated a sermon or two.

If I think back on my 30 years in the pulpit, I wonder what my consistent themes were? I don't know if I know the answer to that. That is perhaps a better question for the people who heard all those sermons. I do know that I ended most every sermon with the phrase, "God desperately loves you. God desperately loves the world. God desperately wants you to love the world and needs you to build a bridge from God to the world." I think people would say that my focus was on reaching people.

Another one of the beliefs that I share often is the concept to "lead with grace." I think I've been consistent with a theology embedder in the Wesleyan and Armenian tradition. Wesleyan theology emphasizes grace, free will and God's providence (rather than God's manipulation). It focuses on the head through intellectual faith, the heart through a personal experience of the Holy Spirit and hands that become the body of Christ for the world. It is a theology that looks to scripture, tradition, experience and reason to make sense of the world. We are a people who have both an intellectual faith and the experience of the strangely warmed heart.

It is important to know your core understanding/beliefs/ practices. If you're not clear on those, your congregation will be in a fog. That doesn't mean everybody needs to agree with you or that everyone needs to follow the same discipleship path. You should know your path.

I would know what I believed.

CHAPTER 22

Take a Step

Take a step; just one step. Saving the world might be above my pay-grade, but in the time I have left, I would try to save my part of the world. As disciples of Jesus, we take seriously that grace is given to us through the sacrament of Holy Communion. In the breaking of the bread and the sharing of the cup, we become the hands and feet of Christ for the world. That, along with the Great Commission, compels us out into the world to share the love of God with others.

If you try to save the whole world, you are stopped even before you take the first step due to the magnitude of the task. However, you can decide what you can do; you can take a step. You can't do everything for everybody. You can select the one thing you can do. Each of us can make a difference!

At the Church of the Shepherd in St. Charles, we decided that we would be the church that responded to disasters in our community. Over time, through our commitment to that ministry, that small step, we became the church that gave away furniture. We didn't have a food pantry, but we did have a warehouse out of which we could distribute furniture to families who had lost everything through a disaster. One small step led to another step. It's like going up a long staircase, one step at a time. It's impossible to go from the bottom directly to the top in one giant leap.

Although, if you take one step at a time, before you know it you have reached the top. What's the one step you can take to try to make the world outside your door a better place?

I might not be able to affect the whole United Methodist Church, but I can affect the one I'm serving. As Bishop, I may not be able to affect the worldwide United Methodist Church, but I can affect the Missouri Conference.

Take a step and focus on it. Stay with it; be consistent.

Take a step.

CHAPTER 23

Jump In!

I would jump in feet first. Invest fast into your people and your community. I think you have to be invested to truly love the people of God. As the song goes, "Here I am, send me, Lord."

I offered myself indifferently to God to be used for his purposes and jumped in headfirst into that work of ministry. As ministers, we sometimes tend to talk about the need for community members to be involved, but have trouble doing what we preach to others. We avoid it by spending all of our time ministering to those who are already in our churches so that we don't have any time to meet someone new or disciple someone or serve those we don't know.

We pastors love to read and study our books and hang out in our offices, hoping people will come to us. It would be nice if everyone came to us, but that's not realistic. Rather than spending all our time studying theology or the Bible, pastors should study the community.

The paid work of what we do is about exegeting the community – studying and learning about who is in your community; where they are, what the need is, who is hungry, where there is housing or lack of housing and what are the community strengths and weakness?

In order to do this, you must go to the schools, talk to school administrators and teachers, get engaged with civic leaders and make connections with social services in your area. Ask them, "What do you need?" and let that guide your own personal service to the community.

This requires pastors to jump in. It becomes truly difficult to learn and understand the community if you do not live in the community; it's not impossible, but it's really hard. If you are part-time or in seminary school, you have other demands on your life during the week that don't allow you to jump into community life as you might want. You must finds ways to jump in anyway.

When I was in seminary, I had three small churches. I learned to jump in through the school (driving the school bus), the fire department, joining clubs, going to baseball games and hanging out in the community. I jumped in.

Jump in and find out what your gifts can do for the community. If you like to teach, substitute teach. If you like to volunteer, volunteer at the library or hospital. Join the city council. Get involved.

This is especially true in small towns where outsiders are sometimes seen with suspicion. It is hard not to like a person who fully adopts the town as their own.

I think it gets harder in the suburbs, because you can feel like a needle in a haystack. You have to pick something and get some focus. In Lee's Summit, even though I joined the fire department,

I discovered that alone didn't get me engaged in the community. The fire department crew knew me, but no one else did. So, I jumped into the Lee's Summit social service agency.

While I was getting out into the community, looking for new people, I would meet families that were really struggling. They needed clothing, food and assistance. I called the county-provided social service agency, but it did a terrible job and could not adequately fill their needs.

It was difficult to understand because this was an affluent community. So, in response to the needs of our community, I along with the director of the agency and some other pastors, started our own social service agency.

This became a place where the church could do good work for our neighborhood. I didn't search for this, but sometimes something picks you. It gives me great pleasure to drive by this agency today and see the work that continues there and to know I was a part of that.

During this time I also helped reorganize, rebuild and refit a fire department. When I first started as fire chief, not one fire truck would start. I towed 16 fire trucks to the junk yard that year. This department was in the habit of taking retired Kansas City fire trucks and when they would no longer run, they would park them behind the building.

When I left, they had a new building, new fire trucks, paid staff and an ambulance. At the time, Grace Church (my appointment) didn't even have a building. We had services in a shopping center and were attempting to start this new church.

In Kansas City, I served as the night chaplain at a research hospital on Friday nights. I got to know all kinds of people and convinced a doctor to come to church. I met a lot of people during my service in this capacity.

Jump into something. Pick a couple of places in which you pour your life. It pays off in growing your own discipleship and builds trust and relationships with the community you are serving.

I would jump in.

———— CHAPTER 24 ————

Don't Go Back

I would not go back to the places I once served. This is absolutely critical. In the United Methodist tradition, we practice itineracy, a Biblically-inspired system for sending pastors to local churches. The typical United Methodist pastor will move multiple times over the course of their ministerial career. Leaving is hard. Staying gone can be even harder. However, when you leave, you need to leave.

Even though it is hard, I wouldn't go back to weddings, funerals or baptisms. That is so hard, especially if you have jumped in and invested, built a life and committed your service to a group of people. Some of those people may have become friends. It's hard to leave friends.

This is such a critical boundary issue that we talk about it every year in multiple ways to the group of clergy and laity who are being appointed or assigned for this work. We talk about professional ethics and remind people that interference in another person's ministry is one of the few chargeable offenses in our shared Book of Discipline.

The reasons against staying gone are more important than simply following the rule to the letter of the law. Every time you go back, it means you are not taking that same time and investing it in the community in which you are now the pastor. I don't think people understand that important clarification. They don't understand why they can't go back to do a funeral, a wedding, a baptism. What's the harm?

In my experience and in my tenure as bishop, I have seen pastors who go back and maintain dinner groups with their five best friends from their former church. It's just dinner, they say, it's not even a worship service or a liturgical moment. They are missing the point. What is wrong with going back socially is that while you are maintaining relationships at your previous appointment, you are failing to invest in five new people at your new context. You are undercutting your ministry in your new location as well as undercutting the pastor who stepped into your previous role.

I have never had any time to go back to my previous appointments because I choose to jump headfirst into the next place. I have gone back to attend the funeral of someone I knew well, but, I didn't preside at the funeral. I might have said a prayer at the request of the incoming pastor, but I didn't perform the service. It is not healthy for the pastor that follows you if you keep going back. It is considered interference. This is true even if the incoming pastor doesn't protest and says they don't care.

When I was at Celeste, a former pastor retired after 15 years of service and bought a farm outside of town where he lived the rest of his life. He did every funeral in town, not just for the Methodists, everybody. You didn't even have to ask who was going to do the funeral, you already knew. This undercut every new pastor who moved into the community. The new pastor did not get to become the pastor of their tribe of Methodists or Baptists or Presbyterians, because he was still acting as their pastor.

You are hurting your colleague in your former church and yourself in your new location by behaving in this way.

We all have to find ways to deal with our feelings of grief and loss. You need to celebrate the memories of what you had, but also be open and ready to experience and create new memories. I think that one of the reasons we go back, is that it's easier than starting over. We simply have not dealt with our own grief over leaving. One of the greatest healers of grief and loss is time. Not that you forget, but things change over time. Most of the time, when you go back, it's not quite the same because those people have gone on to other things. The going back is anticlimactic.

I was just starting out with a new church launch, when one of our young couples lost a baby. I had not experienced the loss of so young a person before because I had never been in a church with young people. As a young father myself, I presided at my first baby funeral. Due to that tragedy and the care I was able to offer that couple, I became this congregation's pastor very quickly. Compare this to my experience in Celeste. Because that retired pastor "came back" it took more time for me to establish myself as pastoral leader for my church. It did not take long for this to change, however, and it came at the cost of another tragedy.

After having only been there for three months, a serious car accident occurred that involved the school superintendent and his family. The father and children perished in this tragedy and the mother was paralyzed. I had never dealt with any kind of tragedy of this magnitude or performed a funeral this large. There were over 1000 people in attendance. I went from the "new kid in town" to "that's our pastor" because I offered pastoral care to the entire community in the midst of that horrible tragedy. If the retired pastor had swept in to conduct the funeral, I would not have been able to become this community's pastor.

The only time I would go back is if the local pastor called and said, "I need you here." I would only go back if it helps or expands that pastor's ministry. Even still, when you do that, you have to be very careful to make sure you redirect attention and say, "That's your pastor."

So, what about your friendships? What do you do about those? You love, celebrate and give yourself permission to grieve the loss. Always remember that church stuff belongs to the incoming pastor. If your friends from a former church contact you, and the conversation leads into church stuff, you must end that conversation immediately and defer to the current pastor. Keep in mind that your colleagues are your brothers and sisters. You are in a fraternity of sorts that urges you to think most generously and graciously about their work and gifts before your own.

Outgoing pastors need to admit that if anything I do might cause a stumbling block for my successor, I need to resist it. This might mean a phone call, visiting, inviting members of your previous congregation to come hear you preach, conducting secret funeral and wedding services so the incoming pastor won't know or inquiring about changes to the life of the local church.

Instead of close friends, perhaps you should have lifetime friends. Lifetime friends are those who you may not see every day, month or year, but who still remain your friends despite the distance or change in situations or circumstances. These lifetime friends can come back into your life over time, but they are in different roles and have different purposes than being in your congregation. They remain lifetime friends and you don't have to go back to keep them.

I would not go back.

CHAPTER 25

Confidence with Humility

I would mix my confidence with a good dose of humility. Confidence without humility is being a jerk. However, humility without confidence often leads to nothing getting done. My confidence can sometimes overrun my humility. At some points in my life, my confidence has been interpreted as being pushy.

As I have become older, I realize I become pushy when I am overly tired, run down and in a hurry. I have also struggled with demonstrating too little humility in my efforts to make change...and fast. My bias toward action drives me to move quickly, sometimes too quickly for others. I have left bodies in the ditch as I have run over them to keep things moving quickly along. Had I more humility, perhaps fewer people would have gotten wounded along the way. I don't regret the result, I regret the hurt along the way.

It's good to recognize that you may not know everything. You may not have all the answers. I'm reminded of the lady at my first church who stood up during my sermon and exclaimed, "You don't know what you're talking about!" This made me mad. Although, looking back on it 30 years later, it's possible that she was right.

I once told a new young member of our staff, "You are going to make some grand mistakes...at least I hope you do."

One of the ways you learn is through failure and mistakes. Mistakes give you immediate failure so you can course correct. I heard a story once about a father and son crossing the country by car through a mountainous region with lots of roads. Heading down the wrong path meant potential danger for the lack of roadside services like gas. On their way back home through the same region, they attempted to follow the same pathway only in reverse. The two came to a fork in the road in which they could not remember which way – was it left or right? After deliberation, they decided to pray for God to show them the way. After prayer, they choose left. The father had not driven 500 yards before they quickly recognized it was the wrong way. He immediately turned around and went down the right road. After some time, the son said, "But Dad, we prayed, why did we go down the wrong road?" The dad said, "Son that prayer allowed us to see sooner rather than later that we have chosen the wrong path. Had we selected the correct path, we would have driven for miles and miles before we were assured we were going the right way."

Mistakes help you determine the right course. They are essential to leadership. I am a big believer in failing fast. In fact, it's one of the principles I try to live out in my new role – how can we become nimbler so that we can fail faster and try something new or fail quickly so we can adjust our strategy and keep momentum moving forward? Recognizing failure gives confidence a good dose of humility.

I don't like failure, but failure teaches you so many things about yourself. It teaches you that you could be wrong. When I was in my 20s, I didn't think I could possibly be wrong. If you arrive at 58 and still think that, something has gone widely wrong. I have noticed that some pastors lack confidence because of a misplaced understanding that confidence is a sin. This seems like false humility to me. We haven't always valued confidence in church work. The Apostle Paul had bouts of too much confidence where he came across the page as being a jerk. He also had bouts of doubt that often drained his confidence. It can be a balancing act between confidence and humility. That said, confidence can be a gift that comes with receiving a call from God and being affirmed in community through your gifts.

The Church needs more confident people. There is a fine line between confidence and being a jerk. Humility is required for leadership. Too much confidence will prevent you from being approved by the Board of Ordained Ministry or from connecting with people in the pew. It can be an unattractive trait that propels people from you rather than to you.

However, humility with little confidence produces a wet rag. You get run over, and you can't go places because people won't follow. From a Cabinet perspective, we hear this from Pastor Parish Relations Committees who tell us their pastor cannot lead. When we have a pastor with confidence and no humility, those same teams will say the pastor is a bully. Confidence mixed with humility is a tricky formula that you can easily mess up. It's no wonder clergy get confused. People want leaders; leaders who practice humility and confidence.

Where do you get confidence? Some of it comes from your DNA, but more of it is from life experiences and having mentors that see something in you, affirm you and guide you. In my case, my church community built up confidence in me. I was an insecure kid who struggled in school, but my church and a community of leaders (including the women of my family through a grandmother, mother and aunt) helped form me into the person I am today. All parents have had to help their children find confidence at times in addition to helping them learn humility. I would invite you to become someone who builds people up, not someone who tears people down. We all know someone who sucks confidence from others versus someone who builds confidence from others. I love Rev. Dr. Roger Ross's saying, "I see something in you." Let us spend our lives seeing something in others and building them up.

I would have confidence with humility.

CHAPTER 26

Ask More Questions

I would ask more questions. As a young person, I was not a question-asker. I wasn't naturally curious. Looking back, I was probably lacking confidence and questioned whether I had a right to learn more. Still, through years of ministry experience and thanks to the mentorship of people like, Lovett Weems, former director of the Lewis Center for Church Leadership at Wesley Theological Seminary, I have learned to ask powerful questions.

Asking questions was central to the work executed through the Healthy Church Initiative (HCI) throughout the state of Missouri and the rest of the country. Questions were at the heart of the process through thousands of conversations with laity and clergy. Questions allowed congregations to discover their present reality rather than simply telling them where they were. It has been my experience that people rarely accept someone else's opinion of their reality. Good coaches and consultants ask powerful questions that allow the participants to see their present reality in a new light.

Church planting consultant Jim Griffith taught me the most powerful question and I have used this question time and time again, "Tell me about a time when..." This is an especially helpful approach when you are working on identifying leaders and helping leaders see the fruit of their ministry. Griffith based this question on his belief that past experience is the greatest indicator of future performance. I think this question works in pastoral situations, too, including pre-marital conversations or missional experiences. When you are coaching people on theological reflection, it is good to start with, "Tell me about a time this past week when you experienced God, felt the most support from your partner, experienced cultural discomfort, or witnessed team-work, etc."

Asking powerful questions and discovering the art of silence are skills that are linked together. Key to asking more questions is coming to terms with the discomfort of silence, rather, the power of silence. Church consultant Paul Borden, author of *Assaulting the Gates, Hit the Bullseye* and *Direct Hit,* taught me skills about using silence. He would say, "Let silence carry the moment." I have had to work hard on this skill.

Clergy have a tendency to want to fill in the silence. Most people are not comfortable with one beat, two beats passing by without some type of noise or talk. We have a tendency to rescue people rather than allowing the silence to envelope the room. Through silence, people have the opportunity to reflect, think more deeply and wrestle with the stuff they are hearing from themselves and others. Resist the temptation to fill in the blank for others. This is true for pastoral conversations, confirmation classes, Bible studies and small groups, funeral preparations, committee work and congregational meetings.

Vocational coaches are typically great at using silence in their sessions to illicit an "owned" response from the coachees. People have to own their answers. Pastors could learn a lot from this approach. Pastors are not meant to be the "Answer Man or Woman." Jesus was good at asking questions (Mk. 10:36, Matt. 16:15, Jn. 21:15) of his disciples. It was part of his teaching method. Pastors could take a page from Jesus' playbook and learn to ask more questions of their people and give them the space and silence to answer for themselves.

Using questions and silence well is key to good leadership. I wish I had learned the skill sooner than later in my ministry. I would have been a better pastor/leader had I learned the art of good questions and the value of space and silence to help people come to their answers on their own.

I would ask more questions.

—— CHAPTER 27 ——

Listen to Outside Voices

I would listen to more outside voices. I have been a Methodist my entire life. It would have been easy to only listen to the voices within our part of the Church. Thankfully, I have learned valuable lessons from different people with different perspectives, including different tribes of Christianity, that changed my ministry and leadership. Through their leadership, they gave me gifts that I still employ today. Left to my own devices, I would not have thought of any of those approaches to ministry and life.

My friend Adam Hamilton taught me the importance of searching beyond our comfort zones for new perspectives and ideas. When we first started our churches in 1990, he said, "Let's go on a road trip and find someone who has started churches. Maybe we can learn something from them."

We spent a couple of weeks traveling around the Midwest talking to pastors who had started churches, asking them questions and seeing how they had shaped a new community of faith for new people. That was a gift.

Adam had already developed a good habit of listening to outside voices. I was a dyed-in-the-wool Methodist, but Adam was comfortable swimming in other pools and learning from them. Had I been left to my own devices, I would have only contacted United Methodist pastors. Adam taught me it was okay to listen and learn from others. He knew that you could pick and choose what was helpful to your context. He knew that much of what these outside-the-tribe leaders were doing had nothing to do with doctrine or belief, but were technical and adaptive techniques for identifying, connecting and communicating with new people. These are good ideas, regardless of where they originate.

Listening to outside voices, even those outside your theological preference or your realm of expertise helps challenge and strengthen what you do believe. And who knows? You may discover that what you thought you knew or believed needed some challenging. For folks in my denomination, I find that it is difficult for them to listen to voices outside the mainline church.

It is so easy to get tunnel vision and to refuse to see beyond your tribe. Outside voices may stretch you and make you uncomfortable. That discomfort is part of the learning process. Who are any of us to say that we have the market on all the right answers? I say anything beyond the Articles of Religion are fair game for questioning. Be willing to adapt and change while at the same time, knowing your core values are unmovable.

If you are going to be effective in your context, you have to talk beyond your tribe. The majority of new people you will connect with will have either a non-Methodist heritage or no Christian heritage at all. If you only know the ways of United Methodism, how will you be able to connect to and translate for other people?

What often stops us is our fear of their theology. You can still learn from someone you disagree with in theology. While theology does inform practical ministry, there are technical opportunities that can be learned from all parts of the world.

In the Missouri Conference, we have recently hired Franklin Covey for some work on implementation of our vision and strategy. They are outside our tribe and they are outside our comfort zone; we have hired them to discover the questions to which we have become deaf and blind. Listening to outside voices helps us understand ourselves better. Who makes you uncomfortable? Who pushes you?

That said, let me insert a warning of a common mistake in which I, too, have been guilty. Sometimes people go off to yet another conference or seminary and bring back an idea and attempt to shove it into their context. The work of reflection and interpretation is key. Leaders have to learn consistency and constancy in their approach to ministry lest they be considered a waffler.

Work has to be done sorting out the material and contextualizing within your setting, determining how it aligns to your vision. What is appropriate to interpret and re-interpret in my context? How can this learning help me in my context?

I would listen to outside voices.

CHAPTER 28

Lead More Than Push

I would lead more than push. People have to look and see for themselves. Leaders are people who have followers. I have often had to remind myself and the leaders I have coached that if you look behind you and no one is there, you are not leading, you're lost!

As I've said before, leading United Methodists is a bit like herding cats. You can't push them. You can't pull them like you would a dog. Cats dig in their claws. You have to coax a cat. It's about invitation. It's the same with sheep, when you push them, they scatter.

There is a reason Jesus uses sheep as his metaphor for people. People and sheep have a lot in common. They respond similarly to leadership. Sheep learn their shepherd's voice. They learn to trust that voice and they respond to the voice when it calls. Congregations know your voice. Use your voice to invite and lead them forward, always checking behind to make sure they are tracking. Occasionally, you will have to go grab one or two, or a growing crowd, and bring them back to the fold.

It's crucial during those moments to revisit your vision. Make sure they know where you are headed, help them learn your voice so they can grow to trust it.

I have tried to push people where I wanted them to go. I'm not saying a little push doesn't hurt once and a while. You might even gently push a cat and gain a little progress, but if you push too hard and that cat doesn't want to go, it will swipe at your hand.

My predecessor, Bishop Robert Schnase, described this using a rubber band. A rubber band's tension is helpful. It makes it a great tool for binding things together. The tension is not the problem, but if you stretch and stretch that band, the tension becomes more than the band can tolerate and it snaps, stinging the hand that stretched it too far.

For every time you push in order to get a result, you have to give five invitations. We know this, right? You always get further with honey than vinegar. One of the great tools for local pastors to use is understanding invitations as "ICNU" conversations.

Pastors should spend a portion of their weekly time meeting with the people in their congregation and broader community and tell them, "I see in you…" (ICNU). Affirm for them the ways in which you see God through the Holy Spirit working in their lives.

What gifts have you witnessed? How have they made their community a better place? What are they doing well in their personal and social lives? People in our world are lacking in affirmation. Invitation and affirmation are connected. Affirm the gifts in someone and invite them to use those gifts for the sake of the kingdom.

The key to this advice is acknowledging our wants and desires regarding controlling the outcome. While I may want to control the result, I have come to realize that I am not in control of the result.

My role in bridging the gap between God and the people

is to offer the invitation. Beyond that, the Holy Spirit and the person are engaged in that work. You may have to offer it again and again. As the old saying goes, you can lead a horse to water, but you cannot make it drink.

As pastors and shepherds, our job is to bring people to the water. We trust that the Spirit will do the rest. I am in control of the invitation so I work on getting better and better at offering the invitation. Learning how to tell the story of others who are responding to the invitation of God through discipleship and leadership helps others respond to their own call.

People need to see how their response will benefit themselves and their family or their community. We do this through telling the stories of transformed lives and communities.

In Missouri, our missional giving as congregations through apportionments continues to rise. This past year, we set another record for payout (the percentage of churches who pay 100 percent of the missional obligations to the general church). I think this is because we have done a better job of showing how that money grows the kingdom and offering the local church tools to help them grow their portion of the kingdom. It's by invitation more than push, though.

Leading is an art, not a science. I've most often fallen off a fence on the pushing side of leadership. At other times, I've fallen off the fence on the invitation side. It takes both invitation and a bit of pushing to get things done. However, I recommend leaning toward inviting more than pushing. You will get further in the end.

Though in the short run, you may feel like you ought to be pushing. Leading by invitation means giving up some control and having some determined patience.

I would lead more than push.

CHAPTER 29

Stretch

I would stretch myself. I would lean in and do some things I don't like to do.

Every job has rent, meaning the tasks that must be completed that you don't like doing. I have never had a job that didn't have rent as part of the workload. Even some things you like have rent.

Recently, while visiting with my grandson, he told me his favorite class in school is PE. He really likes the activities he gets to participate in while in PE class. What he doesn't like to do is the warm up stretching before those activities. It takes time away from the activities that he'd rather be doing; rent.

As I look over the past 40 years, there have been a lot of things I had to do that I didn't want to; things that stretched me. Even now, some of my hobbies require tasks that I'd rather not do. I plant ornamental grasses around my yard. Every year, they must be pruned and separated.

The work is hard and hot and I don't particularly like it. Still, I love to see the new grasses take root and flourish. To stay healthy and fit, I walk three miles every two days. I don't like it, my muscles hate it, but the rent must be paid.

I entered the ministry in a time when technology was

taking off in a big way. During my senior year of seminary, we purchased a computer. Before that, the greatest technological advancement I had experienced was an electric typewriter equipped with an eraser ribbon that would allow you to go back and correct typos. Learning how to use that computer stretched me; it was rent I had to pay. Today, social media dominates the world of communication. I have been slow to learn the ins and outs of social medial, but I am leaning in and learning. You have to stretch yourself and purposefully lean in to the necessary tasks, even if you find them uncomfortable.

When you pay rent, you learn a lot and you can meet people that profoundly change your life. Early in my career, I found myself working as an associate pastor in Greenville, Texas. Several times during this assignment, I thought to myself, "I'm not cut out to be an associate in this church!" My primary job was to organize about 150 youth, the largest group I had ever managed. The rent was much higher than I wanted to pay.

As I look back on this time, I probably learned more about myself in this season of my ministry than any other and I met people who influenced my life and career for years after. Would I go back? No, but, I leaned in, learned a lot and it stretched me.

One thing that has always stretched me is writing. Being in ministry requires that you be able to communicate. You have to be able to write: sermons, letters, articles, books, etc. Even in my current role as Bishop, every week there are requests for information that I must write. For me, writing is rent. If you don't cover the rent, you can't the keep house.

I know pastors who like the platform part of being a pastor, but don't like the work of the pastor. Ministry is not about "liking" every aspect of your work or being comfortable. It's about leaning in and stretching yourself. I've heard pastors say, "I'm not turning in my charge conference paperwork.," or, "I'm not turning in the year-end report. I don't like it."

Who said you were going to like it? When was ministry about liking all of it? Get over it! If you don't like getting out of your office, do it anyway. Go to the Chamber of Commerce meeting, participate in a social justice march, get out in the community. You have to stretch yourself. If you don't like capital campaigns, but your church is in need, do it anyway. In ministry, it's not about being comfortable.

I would pay the rent. Lean in and stretch yourself.

CHAPTER 30

Open Some Windows

I would have fun and open some windows. You have to develop some interests beyond the local church. Why is it such a shock when others see clergy at a baseball game? We clergy have a reputation for not having a life beyond the church. We are too stuffy. We get a reputation of being stuffy because we don't have any interests beyond the church. Find a life beyond yourself and the church. Get some friends who are not church people.

Go fishing, go to a ball game, take a walk or go to a concert. In order to continue to work hard, you better have some fun. I don't want to end my career and have no life. I don't want to be one of those retired ministers who doesn't have anything but the church. I want to have a life and friends beyond the church. In one of my former churches it was said that, "Bob Farr works hard, plays hard and does church hard."

The model for me was Rev. Marie Hyatt, my hometown pastor in Creighton. In those days, she had to work three times as hard as any white male pastor. From her I learned to work hard. Nevertheless, I also learned to play hard. Marie organized a game night at the church and invited people to come play table games. Marie loved table games and she was wildly competitive. She also loved to play pitch and would come to our house to play. She was wicked at it and hated to lose. This part of her character made her real to me. She was a real person with real emotions who could have fun. I discovered she was just another person. Playing games and having fun reveals a bit about people's lives. Marie opened a window into her life through her playing that gave me a glimpse of my pastor as a real person.

Spending hours with a group of people having fun offers opportunities to speak into their lives as well. I took a group of men to Canada for a week of fishing. I learned more about those guys during those days than I ever did in church. Even in our leadership retreats, we always incorporated some play into our sessions. It opened up some windows and allowed us to see more of each other in a different light.

Part of a Sabbath rhythm is play. Jesus seemed to play quite a bit. When Jesus changed the water into wine it was a miracle, but maybe it wasn't all about a theological treatise. Maybe he just wanted to go to a party. After his resurrection, Jesus came back and went fishing. Maybe he just wanted to be out on the boat. Maybe we are over spiritualizing scripture. Don't be so stuffy. You're not that pious or important. Go have fun. Open the window so others can see a different side of you.

What are you playing at? Go play. What do you like to play at? Go play, whatever it is.

— CHAPTER 31 —

Be Generous

I would be generous. I don't want to be laid in my grave and have people think I was stingy. I want to be generous. I learned generosity from my great-grandmother, Clara Farr. She was a preacher's kid. Her dad was a circuit rider in the Dunker Church, a forerunner of The Disciples of Christ Denomination. She didn't have money, but she was gracious with everything she had. Generosity is more of a lifestyle than the amount of money you give, and she was generous with her life. When she worked as a switchboard operator for the town of Adrian, Missouri, she knew everyone and talked to everyone.

She later moved to Hamilton, Missouri where she would stop and talk to everyone she met. She was forever giving away the garden vegetables she raised. She prayed for everyone. From her I learned if you don't give it away when you don't have much, you won't give it away when you have a lot. She gave out candy to anyone who would come in and visit. She reminded me that when you are generous yourself, you can teach others about generosity simply through how you live.

Growing up, I never heard a sermon on money. While serving at my church in Celeste, one Sunday I encouraged the congregation to give for an air conditioning project. At the time, we had a retired Nazarene pastor attending. After my sermon, he approached me and inquired, "How much are you giving, pastor? I'll match you." At the time, I was a seminary student with no money. I was giving what I thought I could. I had grown up in The Methodist Church and at best learned to be a spontaneous giver. In other words, if it moved me, I gave. Now, I was being challenged to take generosity more seriously by a lifetime Nazarene preacher. How do you tell a Nazarene preacher who had preached for 50 years without much of a salary, without much of a retirement and who was being more generous than I, that I couldn't give because I was in seminary? He had learned to tithe and I had not. I had a spiritual crisis. For Susan and I, this was the first time in our lives we had to sit down and make a plan of giving. We looked at what percentage we were at and developed a plan to grow it.

Tithing is the floor, not the ceiling. Most people begin giving through spontaneity off and on, next move on to being regular givers, then tithing and finally on to generous giving. I learned the hard way, don't ask something of your people that you are not willing to do yourself. People see through it; they smell it.

A lot of young clergy say, "I'm spending all this money on seminary, so that's my tithe." Remember that your congregation spent similar money on graduate school, and we expect them to give. Some clergy tend to think that because they give a lot of extra time to the church, they don't need to tithe; again, we expect our congregations to do it. If you preach about tithing, tithe. Give and be generous. I really would like to be known as someone who is generous beyond just tithing. Live generously; all of life!

I would be generous.

CHAPTER 32

Make it Personal

I would make it personal. Remember, this is a people business. If you want to be an effective pastor, you must make it personal or people aren't going to follow you. People don't care how much you know until they know how much you care. As I look back in my ministry, I think this is absolutely true. Caring about the folks in the pews and outside the pews is job one! It's all about relationships, period. Relationships matter and make the difference in whether a ministry is fruitful or not.

When you call people on the phone, they are surprised. When you write a handwritten note, they pay attention. People like to be noticed by their pastor. Do you want to increase your church's attendance on Sunday? Call 20 families on Saturday afternoon and say, "I hope to see you tomorrow." Even if you don't talk to them personally, leave a message. Text someone if that works better.

If you want to get a response out of your people, call them on Sunday night and ask them, "How are you doing?" It has nothing to do with whether or not they were in worship; it has to do with caring.

When I left Church of the Shepherd, someone stood up at the going away party and asked, "How many of you got a note from Bob you couldn't read?" It didn't matter that they couldn't read it, it mattered that I wrote it.

This weekend I texted one of my pastors who was getting ready to be introduced at his new church. He felt cared for.

As a pastor I would do the following every week as a ministry of encouragement:

Send five cards thanking specific people for something they had done. (The bigger your church, the harder it is to keep up with what is going on; you may need someone to help you. My assistant at Church of the Shepherd would prepare and have ready a list of names for these thank you cards.)

Make three telephone calls thanking specific people for their work.

Visit at least one person and take them to lunch. (Why would you ever go to lunch by yourself, when you could be talking to somebody? If you can't find someone to go to lunch with, go to the school and have lunch with the students. Don't ever go to lunch by yourself.)

How are you going to stay connected with people? It doesn't matter if you have 12 people or 1200, how are you going to give a personal touch? This is a people business. Relationships matter.

I would make it personal.

—— CHAPTER 33 ——

Change the Temperature

I would try not to please everyone. Being in ministry is not a popularity contest. If you're going to rate your value or personal worth by the temperature in the room, you are going to have a weary assignment there. Ask yourself, were you put in the room to reflect the temperature around you or change the temperature in the room? The more you try to please everybody, the fewer people you are going to please. I once heard that Billy Graham said he only wanted to hear admiration from one person when he got to heaven; Jesus Christ.

To be in ministry you have to have a pretty high level of tolerance for pain. Be prepared to take some healthy criticism, but don't make it who you are. My whole life I have received anonymous letters from angry people. For me, anonymous letters go in the trash. Don't worry about an anonymous letter. Churches are great rumor mills, and it doesn't do any good to be thin-skinned in ministry. Listen, respond if needed, but don't take it on and make it personal.

Jesus criticized things and he took a little criticism. Jesus turned over the moneychangers in the temple and he didn't mince any words when he said, "My house was designed as a house of prayer; you have made it a hangout for thieves!" (Matt. 21:13) Neither did Jesus mince any words when he told Peter, "Get behind me, Satan." (Matt. 16:23) Jesus experienced criticism every week of his ministry. Jesus spent Holy Week being criticized by others. Jesus experienced a large crowd of people who turned against him. Jesus knew what it was like to stand at his darkest hour by himself. He did not let it change his core being.

At churches I have served, I have had people come up to me and say, "I was prepared not to like you." Or, "I like you, but I don't like what you say." Maybe that means I'm staying true to myself.

I want people to like me as much as anybody else. I'm a people-guy. I enjoy their company. I don't give up on people very easily. I try to follow the Matthew 18 principle and I want to sit down with people I disagree with; but this is not about pleasing everyone. This is about staying true to yourself and your calling.

People have publicly left every church I have served. I cannot be the pastor everybody wants. Over time, I have learned to understand that's not as a personal slight. You will not be able to relate to some people and some people will not be able to relate to you. Sometimes when people cannot relate to you, they need to worship somewhere else for the sake of their own spiritual growth. You have to be self-differentiating enough to understand someone else's motives apart from your personality. There is no way to please everyone. I've also learned sometimes it's simply a season in someone's life that needs a change and they need someone else to blame it on. As pastors we are an easy target. It's okay... I've had to learn it's going to be okay. There are seasons in our lives, churches lives' and ministry. Sometimes, people just need a change. Don't take it personally.

At my first church, one Sunday during my sermon, a

woman stood up, pointed her finger and stated, "You do not know what you are talking about!" I grew up in a church that didn't so much as say, "Amen," let alone speak back to the pastor during the sermon. I gripped the pulpit and before I could reply, another woman stood up and said, "Just sit down, shut the hell up and let the boy talk." If I was shocked by the first comment, the second comment did me in. I don't remember anything else from that morning. The next thing I do remember is calling my district superintendent from my mother's house.

It's a misnomer thinking that ministry is a safe place to do life. It's actually quite risky, especially in today's world. If you're entering ministry today, it has to be on purpose.

You have to know who you are and what God has called you to do. Nonetheless, you cannot barrel down the road in disregard of others. You are not the only one called and you're not the only one with an opinion. The most fruitful pastors are not authoritarian, but they are purposeful. It's not about being popular but you must have purpose. Try not to run over people, though, with your purpose.

Over the course of one year or 40 years in ministry, you will hear criticism. Some of it will be deserved; most of it is simply people spouting off. Don't take it on. This is not a popularity contest. If all you do is annoy people, you will not have a healthy ministry. Some pastors say, "As long as I'm doing God's work, I'm fine." It might be healthier to think that God could be sending you people to help you see a different path. You do need people to like you, but if your goal is to make everyone happy, it will have you chasing your tail. This is a balancing act. Your goal is to follow your purpose and calling. Healthy criticism won't hurt you, but not all criticism is helpful.

Don't try to please everybody. Change the temperature in the room, don't let the temperature change you.

I would try not to please everyone.

— CHAPTER 34 —

Dream

I Would Have a Dream Project. When I arrive at a church, it doesn't take me long to have a dream project in mind for that church. I start thinking about how to revive the church, the community or the area. I begin to see beyond the current reality.

If you can't see beyond the current reality, the people will not be able to see it either. Church people already know the current reality so there's no need to restate it without casting hope for the future.

Sharing current reality without casting forth a dream is cruel. Understand the reality, but be ready with a dream for the future even if they are small dreams. Most people give the pastor the benefit of the doubt and want to be supportive; this is their moment of possibility, too. Everyone should have a dream for their church and what it can be, so be prepare for some people who want to be supportive and some who do not.

Dreams can begin to be fulfilled with little victories. In one country church I served, we upgraded from a hand-cranked mimeograph machine (1978) to an electronic one. It was the first new thing this congregation had purchased in years. Our Saturday nights became different. Instead of ruining white shirts making bulletins, we drew a crowd just to watch the electronic machine spit out the bulletins in record time. This one small accomplishment gave the church hope to dream for bigger things. Small wins begin to restore confidence in your people.

I always want to leave a church better than I found it. I always want to leave more church than I had on arrival. That same small open country church went from 18 to 60 people in attendance in 3 ½ years. I did this by driving my car up and down the country roads and knocking on doors, and, getting one small win at a time.

Have a dream even if it's small to start with, but dream of a new reality. If you don't dream it as pastor, how will they?

At one church in Kansas City, the church was in the middle of the neighborhood. It had four roads leading to it; all dead ends. We put up six directional signs and people still couldn't find it. In an effort to play on this negative aspect, we adopted a new slogan, "Best Kept Secret in Kansas City."

The church grew from 50 to 150 people. Today, the building is still there. However, the church is now closed. This drives me crazy. If you look around the neighborhood, there are still people, and the neighborhood is relatively the same with a local elementary school still full of kids only two blocks away. Dreams must be renewed every few years or the church dies.

It's important to mention that sometimes laypersons are the best dreamers. At one church, we were trying to relocate the church building. We had looked at 6 different locations. None of them worked.

It was beginning to look like there was no way to relocate

this church. Then one day, one of the lay people picked me up and had me look out where the new highway was being built. He said, "Right here is where we need to build this church."

He pointed at the all the subdivisions and said, "We need to reach those people." When I looked at the property listing I exclaimed, "They want nearly 6 million dollars for this piece of property!" The lay person looked at me and asked, "Have you knocked on their door and asked what they would take for it?" I had not. So, we went directly to the owner.

The lay person asked her, "Have you ever imagined a church on this hill?" Her reply? "Yes, what would you pay?" When we offered her a price, she said, "I believe we can figure this out." The lay person helped me imagine. He had bigger dreams than I. I'm glad I listened to him. Dreams can appear from any direction.

In the re-naming of Simon, "Simon, thou art Peter," (Matt. 16:18) Jesus had a dream for Peter. He saw something different in Peter and imagined a new life for him. If you cannot drive up to a new place and imagine a new future, what are you doing? Can you imagine a new way? Can you imagine people here?

Can you imagine that one day there will be more people than before? Can you imagine that more people will connect with Christ? Can we imagine a world where this town is better because of us? If you don't have a dream for the place you have been called to, maybe you're in the wrong place. Get a dream; it leads to hope which leads to changed lives.

Currently, in the United Methodist Church, we suffer from a lack of imagination of what could be. We cannot possibly imagine what a new United Methodist Church would look like. Dream a little and see what could happen. It doesn't need to look the same, it just needs to be focused on people and Christ.

I would have a dream.

— CHAPTER 35 —

Teach the Bible

I would teach the Bible. So many of the churches I served did not have an active Bible study when I first arrived. It didn't take long for me to start one. I always taught a Bible study as a pastor in each church I've served. When I taught the Bible, I preached better and was better able to contextualize my sermons. When I taught the Bible, it made the week better and it made life go better.

When you teach the Bible at your church, you get the opportunity to hear stuff outside your own head. You gain a better understanding of what goes on in the small group dynamics of that congregation and you get to know the people better. When you study together, it connects the work you're doing in another areas of the church. Now, it's important to learn how to allow people to start and stop; to get in and then get out of your Bible study so it doesn't feel like a lifetime assignment.

Start out with four to six week studies; then take one or two weeks off and start again. This allows new people a chance to get in and get out. I loved doing Bible studies out of the church building, at coffee shop, mall or workout facility. When your Bible study is out in the public, others want to join in and see what you are doing. It's also great for meeting new people.

If I have a regret, it's that I neither led nor promoted the Wesley style bands, class meetings or transformational small groups (a group focused on practices). If I were to be a pastor again, I would introduce Wesley bands or class meetings that emphasize faith and life practices.

I would focus on the Methodist faith practices as they relate to the individuals' lives. I would give them homework and make them read. I would ask them to tell me about a time they recently experienced God. I would want my Bible studies and small groups to lead people to spiritual transformation, not just study.

In a world that is Biblically illiterate, people are ripe for hearing the word of God. They are starved for Good News. They want to know if God is real and if they can experience God themselves. They want to know if they can go out and practice the Good News themselves.

I would teach the Bible.

── CHAPTER 36 ──

Read the Bible More

I would read the Bible more, not for sermon prep, not for Bible study, but to be immersed in the Word. Although, I have never had much luck sitting down and reading straight through. I tend to read the Bible in spurts and through devotional reading.

I have also learned to pray the Bible. I read three scriptures and pray them over and over before I leave them for the day. I meditate on that one scripture and let it repeat over and over and over in my head. This scripture holds me through the day. It doesn't really matter what your approach is as long as you're reading the Bible, and reading it for yourself. All scripture applies everywhere, all the time and it is one of the best gateways to spending time with God.

I didn't grow up reading the Bible. I've only read from cover to cover once in my whole life; a really difficult task for me. Rather, I see the Bible as a library and I tend to read a book at a time. I jump around throughout the Bible marking scriptures as I go!

My Grandmother O'Neal's Bible was full of hand written notes in the margins. They were fun to read and I hope when I die someone will get a kick out of my notes written inside my Bible.

One of the greatest tools for improving my reading time has been my smartphone. The apps I've installed tell me when it's time to read my Upper Room devotional and scripture reading. Left to my own devices, I would just read. My phone also helps me read a variety of passages. With no direction, I would just read the parts I like, not the ones I don't like. Yes, there are parts of the Bible I just don't like! Whether this is guilt or a gift of God, I am much better at scripture reading since the smartphone entered my life.

Although I grew up believing all scripture applies to all things at all times, I have learned that some scriptures apply specifically to certain situations or seasons of life. I find myself rereading the 23rd Psalm, Matthew 22:37-39 and Romans 8:35. I find myself rereading The Great Commandment, The Great Compassion and The Great Commission passages.

When you read the Bible, you find the things that really speak to you over and over. Memorize them. You may need them in the future when you forget your Bible or when you get old and cannot read. It's been amazing what Christians remember both in scripture and song when they reach their death bed.

I would read the Bible more.

— CHAPTER 37 —

Rest

I would sleep more. I think the ability to sleep well is a gift. My wife has the gift of sleep and can fall asleep nearly anywhere, at any time. I struggle with sleep. On good nights, I tend to get 6-7 hours of light sleep. My wife thinks I sleep lightly because of thirty-one years of fire service and waiting for the phone to ring or fire pager to go off. I have to monitor my sleep carefully, or I don't rest well or often enough.

In an article some time ago, I read that most Americans who wake up in the middle of the night, wake around 3 a.m. I have been waking up at 3:10 my whole life. I have learned to place a pen and paper next to the bed so if I have a sermon or project idea when I wake, I can jot it down before I go back to sleep.

In the Old Testament, most dreams and visions came at night. For example, in I Samuel 3, God calls to Samuel in the middle of the night.

When you're tired, it effects everything else in the day. When I'm tired I tend to be short-tempered, pushy and make snap decisions. When I look back on ministry, I wonder if spiritual desert times were simply lack of good sleep that may have caused a blockage to the spirit-filled life.

During our episcopal orientation, one topic they covered was about resting well. If you're not "putting things away" it can interrupt your sleep. One of my episcopal colleagues told me his wife asked during appointment season, "who are you sleeping with tonight?" She was referring to his tossing and turning over the clergy appointments being made. He wasn't putting things away and it was interrupting his sleep. Now I have the same problem at times. Learning how to develop routines to "put things away" so you can sleep is a key to ministry. One of those routines is rest.

Rest does not always include sleep, but rest cannot replace sleep. However, it is necessary to improve your quality of sleep. Rest is a break from your normal pattern of activity and allows your mind and spirit to renew from the everyday strain.

Rest is a part of Sabbath and it can deeply affect one's spirituality. Each day needs a time of rest. Where is your 15-30 minutes of rest during the day? Just take a simple break from the normal day's work. Rest is so important. A routine of rest is critical. What is your rhythm of rest and Sabbath? How do you put things away? It is important to remember, that coming back from your 'rest' more tired than when you left, is not rest. If you're not resting well, you're not going to sleep.

I would sleep and rest (truly rest) more.

— CHAPTER 38 —

Show Up

I would get out of bed and show up. I grew up with a very strong work ethic. My mother was a hard worker. My dad was a workaholic. He was either working or sleeping. There was no play. Even though I like to play, I learned my work ethic from him. My overall success as a pastor in the early years was not about what I knew, but more about my enthusiasm and my hard work. Hard work and enthusiasm can overcome many other barriers.

If you want to be fruitful in ministry you must have a good work ethic. I don't know many successful pastors who work less than 60 hours each week. If you're looking for a 40-hour check-in, check-out type of ministry, this isn't for you.

Some of our young pastors ask, "Why would I want to be a United Methodist in this season with attendance steadily dropping?" It's a good question! My answer is that you have to be a little crazy and you must want to lead a revival! Pastors need to get up every day and discover a new future for the church because the old ways of the church are gone.

This is not easy when most of our churches have lost their confidence in being the church and are stuck. Friends, any good cause takes more than a lifetime to pull off. Get out and do your best. I've endured what seems like a lifetime of losing seasons as a Kansas City Royals fan, but I still love the game. They finally won their second World Series in 2015 and this gives me hope for The United Methodist Church. Just because the United Methodist Church isn't what it used to be, doesn't mean there isn't ministry that still needs the United Methodist Church. There are new people ready to experience the Wesleyan way of life in the 21st Century. Ministry is a marathon, not a sprint. This is not going to be easy, but it never was. Much of the work we do does not wrap up quickly. Results are not seen quickly.

One of my staff members speaks of the "speed of Church." As a 2000-year-old entity, the Church has a longer view of the world than other not-for-profits or secular organizations. Anything that matters is going to take a lifetime of work – in fact some people would say that anything worth working for is going to take more than one lifetime.

One of our pastors experienced a 15-year process to relocate buildings from a downtown location to a newly developed area of a growing suburb. The congregation had been in existence for over 100 years before talk of relocation even began. Since the expansion, they have seen 300 more people join. The pastor worked hard and endured much criticism. Yet he had many other voices on board to support the dream and see a new future.

It was a long, hard journey and he has outlived some of the naysayers. As of today, the church has pushed attendance toward 2,000 in worship. Church is a marathon, not a sprint, to accomplish a vision.

You have to have some grit. You need to wake up every day, be enthusiastic and be determined to make a difference in people's lives. I always wake up excited about the cause – offering Jesus to others and connecting people to the

Wesleyan way of Christianity.

This isn't just a job. It's a vocation, a way of life. If you are a pastor, there is never a time when you're not the pastor. If you are a lay person there is never a time when you are not a disciple. There is never a time where people see me outside of the church and say, "There's Bob, and he's not the pastor right now." This is about identity. Now, it's not my only identity but it's certainly who I am in Christ.

I would get out of bed and show up.

CHAPTER 39

Experience

You don't know what you don't know.

The Church is global. My first trip out of the country was to India in 1987. As we flew into the airport, I noticed all the thatched and tin roofs built right up against the fence surrounding the airport. This was my first time to truly witness poverty on a dramatic scale.

In Kansas City or Dallas where I went to Divinity School, I had seen poverty. I thought I understood poverty. We rode a bus from the airport into downtown New Delhi. When we stepped off the bus, we were immediately surrounded by hundreds of children. I was overwhelmed by the poverty and astounded by the joy they seemed to have in their lives. You don't know what you don't know.

While in India, some of the visiting clergy were asked to preach Sunday morning. I was asked to preach the 7 a.m. service. I was the youngest clergy on the trip and in my limited experience I was feeling a bit slighted that I would preach the early service.

In Missouri, a 7 a.m. service would have very few people in worship. I was picked up at 5 a.m. and delivered to the parsonage where we sat drinking tea and talking. As time passed, I wondered when we would head over to the church.

The next thing I knew, it was 7 a.m. I looked at my watch and asked, "Don't we need to go to the church?" The pastor of the church answered, "We will go when we need to." As the minutes ticked by, in my western mindset, I kept thinking to myself, "What are we doing?"

I asked two more times about going to the church. The third time I asked, several minutes after worship was scheduled to start, he answered, "It's time to go." When we arrived, I was shocked by what I saw. The church was packed! People were everywhere! There were even people hanging out of the windows. None of this matched my Missouri experience of church. I wondered why in the world there were so many people at the 7 a.m. service.

I learned that the majority of people in India walked to church services, some as far as 6 to 10 miles. Rather than walk to church in the heat of the day, most chose the earlier service so they could walk in the cool of the morning. You don't know what you don't know.

I would encourage everybody to go on mission trips. A mission trip expands your horizons. You experience a church and people you will not experience anywhere else. Every town in the United States has poverty and we cannot ignore that. However, the poverty in some of our developing countries is much deeper.

Until you experience it, you don't have a true understanding or sense of the depth of it. It's easy to be comfortable in our own surroundings and think that this is how everybody lives, or this is how everybody does church. You're doing church one way when there might be 29 different ways of doing church, and each way is a good way. You don't know what you don't know.

There is much to learn. Mission trips allow us to develop

mutually beneficial and inter-dependent relationships. They can teach us something about who we are, and maybe remind us of our interconnectedness. They can also help us build bridges across differences and create mutual accountability for one another. We cannot forget any of the folks who are struggling in the US or in foreign countries. Don't forget the children in our United States downtown metropolitan areas or in our rural communities. Also don't forget the children in Mozambique, Sudan or Beijing.

You don't know what you don't know

—— CHAPTER 40 ——

Saints

I would keep a few saints around. In every church you are going to serve as a pastor, there are people who are ready to help you and do the work of the kingdom. Among all the people who may not be as helpful as they could be, I have always had the privilege of finding with some who did get it. What does it mean to 'get it'? They understand the mission of the church is to reach people for Christ and transform the world.

They understand it's not about them. They showed up to open the door and stayed around to close the door. They have been there from the beginning. They are rarely the loudest or strongest in leadership and sometimes you don't even realize they are one of the saints. In hindsight, they stand out as the true saints of the church. These are people you want to hang around with. They are the encouragers. They are the true voices of reason. They get the mission.

In every church I have served, I could name people who were willing to do what it took to get things done. I could also name those who didn't. It drives me nuts when pastors say, "There is nobody here that gets it." That's not true.

There is always somebody who gets it. You may have to look for them or you may have to discover them; but they are there – salt of the earth people. They do the work. They are always committed to the purpose and strive to follow Jesus each and every day, even when it is hard.

Saints are those people who hang with you even when they disagree with you. They keep showing up. They are always helpful. These people may become a part of your saintly canon. You want to model your life after people like these. You realize how blessed you were to get to work with them.

However, you don't have to meet a saint for a saint to be an influence in your life.

The Apostle Paul, John Wesley, Francis Asbury, Harry Fosdick, Mother Teresa and Billy Graham all became saints in my life. They were a part of my picture, of how or who I wanted to be like. I wanted to preach like Billy Graham, to have the spirit of Mother Theresa, to write sermons like Harry Fosdick, understand theology like John Wesley and have the determination of Francis Asbury.

Saints are the voices that speak to you over the course of your life and ministry. They can be people you have studied, read about or seen from a distance. Keep a few good saints around. For every time you have to hang around someone disagreeable, go hang around some saints.

The scriptures remind us of a great cloud of witnesses around us at all times. Some have gone before us and some are hanging around us right now!

I would keep a few saints around.

— CHAPTER 41 —

Make Meetings Matter

I Would Make Meetings Matter. Lord, how many meetings have I been in over the course of my ministry? I have spent more time in meetings than any single thing I've done in my entire life. Meetings are not my favorite thing to do; can you tell?

Unfortunately, they are a necessary evil. You cannot make progress without an occasional meeting. Even Jesus went to meetings and called a few meetings. On the other hand, you can have a lot of meetings and not make any progress. It's easy to have meetings that don't matter or to lose control of a meeting and go sideways.

There are keys to a good meeting:

- Have an agenda.
- Set a specific start and stop time and stick to it.
- Know the purpose of the meeting.
- Keep it moving and redirect folks back onto the agenda when they go off chasing rabbits.
- Don't leave the meeting without clearly defining next steps and determining what needs to be communicated to the church or other committees.

• Don't be held to the habit of meeting. Don't meet if you don't have to meet.

• End early if the work is done.

• Take breaks.

• Be careful not to have so many meetings that you can hardly remember what you discussed in any one meeting.

Another way to improve meetings is to turn them into small groups. Include a learning piece, devotion time and a praying time. Halfway through my ministry I realized that meetings could also become small groups. I've always heard people say, "I don't have time to participate in a small group because of committee obligations."

Turn your committee work into small groups. Doing this gives your committee work more purpose. If your meetings are only about business and decisions, you are bound for a difficult time. Use them as an opportunity for a chance to grow in faith.

You might as well go to the Rotary Club if your meeting doesn't include any dimensions of spirituality, even if you have made some good decisions. Fellowship and spiritual dimension can take a meeting from "just a meeting" to a meeting with purpose. If a meeting is necessary, make sure it matters.

I would make meetings matter.

— CHAPTER 42 —

Set High Expectations

I would set high expectations. The United Methodist Church, by and large, is not a high expectation church. If you come a little bit and give a little bit, you have the right to say a whole lot. Pastors know that high expectation cultures grow churches, but our fear is that if we set high expectations, no one will come. It's not easy to set high expectations in a church culture of low expectations. You cannot do it by wishing them into existence. It takes lots of time and investment in leadership to begin the culture change.

At Church of the Shepherd, I decided to separate church membership classes from confirmation. Parents lost their minds! Historically, they expected that the end goal of confirmation was joining the church. However, I think, the actual expectation of confirmation graduates is being a disciple. Confirmands need to believe in Jesus Christ. In my opinion, that doesn't require you to be a member of the church. I quickly found out I was alone in this idea. The kids loved it. It allowed them to confirm that they believe in Jesus, without the added responsibility/expectation of joining the established church. If and when a person decided to join the church, they must complete two additional classes.

This is an example of changing expectations. Membership becomes leadership and requires extra steps to fully

understand what it means to be a member of the church
and the expectations of that membership. It took some time
to make this happen. Changing expectations takes time as
pastor. If you're not careful, you may find yourself on the
outside looking in if you haven't done the up-front work.

In 1996, I journeyed to Saddleback Church to see how
they did church and learn from their founding pastor Rick
Warren. He had five things that he required before you could
be considered to serve on the church board:

- Attend

- Participate in a mission trip

- Tithe

- Lead something inside the church

- Lead something outside the church

I came home and imposed these new ideas on my
church board only to have most of the leaders resign their
positions. I hadn't done the front work to change the culture
of low expectations inherited from the Methodist Church.

Use caution, though, if you try setting high expectations at the start of your ministry, you will meet with resistance. Yet the work is necessary because our "low expectation" culture has not helped our churches and we are seeing
a lot of 'dones'. These are the folks who have said "I'm done"
because they have been overextending themselves for the
sake of the low expectation crowd. Burnout for one group
of people provides a shallow understanding of discipleship
for another group of people who let the others carry the
majority of the leadership load. Over time, most people but
not all, will rise to the expectation and create a stronger and
larger core of leaders who can help end the low expectation

culture that exists in our churches. I would set high expectations starting with myself and slowly raise the level of expectations of all people attending our churches. We must move our folks from cultural Christianity to disciples of Jesus Christ. Remember you might become smaller before your church becomes bigger. Bigger without deeper doesn't matter. It takes both to be a fruitful church body of Christ.

I would set high expectations.

CHAPTER 43

Understand Culture

I would understand the culture. You would do well to understand the culture before imparting your strategies. I wish I would have learned, sooner than later, that culture eats strategy for breakfast. Many a good plan has failed because I did not understand the culture. I didn't understand this idea for a large part of my ministry. If I were to do it again, I would do a better job of trying to understand the culture I'm walking into before I tried to change that culture. I made the great mistake of giving out my list of changes right off the bat, only to have the changes die before the second meeting because I didn't understand the culture.

Even if you have practical, reasonable, obvious reasons for the changes, you can't just go in without understanding the local culture and give them your "how to's." If you do, your changes will fail every time.

I heard Jim Ozier, Director of Congregational Excellence, North Texas Annual Conference say once, "pastors are the chief culture crafters of the church." Yes! That is absolutely correct. We spend 90% of our time crafting or re-crafting a church culture into a certain direction, and we fail because we do not understand the culture we are trying to re-craft. If I had it to do over, I would focus on behavioral change over strategies.

If strategy gets eaten by culture, bad preaching will fail every time to communicate the vision you hope to achieve. A vision that connects to scriptures, and understands the culture has the highest possibility of bringing about change. In many of my other books, I share that it is very hard to bring change in a local church without being able to preach it. I inherently knew it, but when I began to understand that we are culture crafters, I really understood how preaching is imperative in crafting new culture in a church. I have seen pastors with great ideas and solid strategies but failed in their ability to communicate any of it through the lack of good preaching.

It takes good communication, interpersonal skills and an understanding that all of these things together help recraft culture. In his book, Canoeing the Mountains,11 Todd Bolsinger identifies three centers of circles. I might call them circles of influence. The first is Technical Competence. My understanding of technical competence is that you first need to demonstrate your competency of doing the basics before a congregation will let you do something they don't understand. The second circle is Influence. You need to demonstrate your love for them and be in relationship with them before they will let you try to talk them into something they don't understand. The third circle, Adaptive Capacity can only be used after you have demonstrated technical competence and you are in relationship with them. They can then give you room to adapt new culture.

Years ago I read a book about change. It used an analogy of a mouse guiding an elephant through the jungle. The basic premise of the book stated that emotions overrule practical, reasonable decisions. In church work the elephant

11 Tod Bolsinger *Canoeing the Mountains* Intervarsity Press (2015)

in the room is emotions and the mouse is practical reason. Since the elephant (emotions) is so large, it finds it difficult to see the small mouse (reason) to follow it out of the jungle. It is the same in our churches; they find it difficult to rationalize change in the face of their emotions. Emotions drive people and often are what make decisions.

A new set of eyes in a new place gives an opportunity for change. Pastors think if we can give it just cause and show them what's obviously the rational thing to do, it will be easy. Unfortunately, the folks who are there can't see it because they have become accustomed to the local culture. So unfruitful ministries, changes to the building, new classes or any kind of change is difficult to implement even though it is the practical thing to do. The elephant in any church culture is emotion.

I would understand the culture.

—— CHAPTER 44 ——

Repeat Stuff

I would repeat stuff. We don't repeat well. In my training as a pastor, I was taught that you didn't want to repeat something; you needed a different theme every Sunday. If you repeated something, you didn't do your homework, you hadn't prepared or you weren't creative enough.

We were taught that every year you needed to come up with new things in order to be fruitful. Then, I went to a Rick Warren seminar and he suggested repeat, repeat and repeat until they get it. He suggested that some things were so important they must be repeated over and over and over.

Pastor Rick Warren is from Saddleback Church which began during the mid-1990's. Saddleback grew to one of the largest churches in America and still is today.

He suggested that successful people in business, not-for-profits and churches understand the value of repeating things like words, values, concepts, themes and ideas over and over so people will eventually remember. It's changed my understanding of leadership and how to communicate within a church.

In an Andy Stanley seminar I attended in the mid-2000's, he pointed out again that, "too often pastors wonder why a congregation doesn't understand the vision."

The pastor might say, "They just don't get it" casting blame on the congregation and leadership. Andy says, it's not their job to "get it." It's our job to communicate it. Remember that every time you communicate vision to the people, things get in the way. "Monday comes in most people's lives." I wish I had known this earlier in my career because I did a lot of blaming people for not getting it when all along I wasn't communicating it enough.

At Church of the Shepherd, I developed a "vision Sunday" that was my time to repeat the four to five things that were really important over the year. It was the "here's where we're headed" day, the "rally the troops" day. One of the things that really reminded me of this happened in Bishop Schnase's seventh year. I went to him and said, "I am sick to death of the five practices! This is all we ever talk about."

That very week, I was in a one of the Missouri Conference's local churches and a member said to me, "You know what, there's this new thing called "Five Practices" and it's the greatest thing!" I was stunned, we had been doing that for seven years!! I went back and told Bishop Schnase what had happened and said, "I guess we had better keep repeating if we want this to get through to our people." In order for the people in the pews to "get it" the leadership has to be sick to death of whatever you're trying to communicate.

We are scared to repeat stuff for fear it will become boring. Still, there are some things you need to hear over and over again; things that are so important that they must be told every month, every year. For example, the Easter story and the Christmas story. Yes, I know there are only so many ways you can unpack these stories. Trust the stories, they are incredible. They have been repeated for 2000 years and are still worth telling again. What are the other five to six stores that need repeating every year in your church? The mission and the vision must be repeated and repeated in order for it to stick. Your values and practices must be repeated over and over if you want them to stick. These are the rocks in the river that provide solid footing as we cross.

After 38 years of marriage, Susan would be disappointed if I only told her, "I love you" on our wedding anniversary. She and I need to hear it over and over again. It's so important it has to be retold and retold for both the hearer and the teller.

What are those things that you need to repeat over and over and over? What are the five things that you want your congregation to be or do? What are the four or five things that are so important in your church, you must tell them over, and over, and over, and over and over?

I would repeat stuff.

CHAPTER 45

Complain Less

I would complain less. In my 40 years of ministry I have noticed that when clergy get together, our tendency is to have Whine and Cheese. We whine about our churches, the system, the conference, the general church and the people in the church. Then, we have some food. All that whining and complaining (and I've done my share of it) hasn't achieved a thing other than to discourage us all the more.

I would complain less. It is counterproductive to everybody's spirit and it's catching, like the flu. The next thing you know, everyone is doing it. Remember what your mom said, "If you can't say something nice, don't say anything at all!" Complaining breeds resentment; it's toxic. You can't pastor a people you resent. Not to mention that when you start whining about your congregation, it gets back, especially with today's social media. Yes, you need a place to unload and vent, but you need to be cautious about selecting the arena in which to do that. Remember, you are never not a pastor.

There are two approaches you can take in ministry: I get to or I have to. I get to be helpful or I have to be helpful. I get to take out the trash, or I have to take out the trash. I get to go to the hospital, or I have go to the hospital. I get to open the door, or I have to open the door. One of our pastors once

commented, "I'm tired of hearing pastors say, 'I have to…'
I'm going to say, 'I get to.'" After 40 years of ministry let me
just say…I get to. It's a privilege to be a pastor in the United
Methodist Church.

Remember you are not that different than the people
you serve. Your education and credentials give you a special
privilege that you should hold with care. People let us into
their very lives at some of the most critical moments. Trust
me, it's a privilege. I would complain less. You shouldn't be
the only one taking out the trash, but if you're unwilling
to take out the trash, you shouldn't be in the pulpit. I truly
believe that our best pastors don't think they are any better
than the people they serve. Be the model, do what needs to be
done. However, if you're the only one taking out the trash,
you might be creating a codependency problem. Don't forget
ministry is about doing it together. Be a multiplier not a
nursemaid. We are to equip the saints but not be or think
ourselves above the saints.

I have always felt very privileged that people actually pay
me to do a vocation that I want to do. I have a job that is my
vocation, rather than having a job that supports my vocation. My role, my credentials, do not give me special privilege. I would rather be remembered as the person who went
to clean out a house after a flood or tornado, than be remembered as the Bishop. I would rather be remembered serving
than supervising. I would encourage more, uplift more, smile
more and…

I would complain less.

— CHAPTER 46 —

Multiply

I would multiply. In the United Methodist Church, we the pastors are ordained to "equip the saints" but not to do their work for them. The church does not need nursemaids or micromanagers. Everywhere I see a pastor act as a nursemaid or micromanager, it ruins the church. That debilitates it and prevents spiritual growth. The problem is, the congregation loves you for it. If you're not careful they will reward you for it, too.

Other times, it can lead to resentment. Either way it's not a healthy way to be in ministry. A go-fetch pastor is not the body of Christ and is not healthy behavior for anybody. Yet, so many congregations think pastors are there to serve them and if there is any time left over, they may serve the wider community. This has led to dying congregations and spiritually dying pastors.

I'm not saying pastors should not do things. I'm saying they should do ministry together with the congregation. Pastors should never do anything by themselves. In my ministry I made uncountable trips to hospitals for visits. In hindsight, I should have taken more people with me. Multiply; that's the name of the game.

We are called to be multipliers. There is a reason Jesus sent out disciples two by two. Don't do anything by

yourself. This can apply to almost anything you do. If you're
going on a hospital call, who are you taking with you to
help teach? Who are you pouring into? Who are you discipling? Who are you investing in, both inside and outside the
church? One model for multiplication is do, recruit, teach,
train, deploy and coach. Then start over. There is another
model from an old periodical called "Group Magazine" that
goes like this:

- I do it, you watch, we talk
- We do it together, we talk
- You do it, I watch, we talk
- You do it, another watches, we talk

By practicing these models, you multiply your ministry
and give others a chance to become disciples.

I would multiply.

CHAPTER 47

Make Friends

I would make friends with community decision-makers In every community I have moved into, one of my first steps is to figure out who are the influencers beyond the church in that community. Some of my first contacts were those 'influencers.'

I started with the obvious ones: school superintendent, principals, the mayor, social service agencies, the sheriff, the chief of police and the postmaster. I asked them to tell me about their community. (I asked the postmaster if I could ride around with the mail carrier. Postal carriers have an excellent grasp on the community.)

I wouldn't do this just once. I made it my habit to go back and visit with them again on a regular basis. At the end of our time together, I always asked, "Is there anything I can be in prayer for in your life?" When you do that, it opens up a door. I've never had anyone say, "No, don't pray for me."

If you want to have influence in the community, you have to know the influencers. My experience was that over time, these people became some of my best friends. They were often facing the same types of challenges and understood the loneliness of being a leader. Most decision-makers are just like everyone else, but being in leadership roles, they have to be careful about everything they say and do.

Making connections is more difficult in larger communities, but it still matters. At The Word at Shaw in the city of St. Louis, our pastor Keith Scarborough made friends with the business owners and managers surrounding the church property.

When it came time to remodel the building, Keith had already made connections with the mayor, city council persons and with his neighbors. As a result of those connections, he was able to avoid the thousands of dollars it would have cost to understand and meet the occupancy requirements for the remodel. One conversation in friendship, leads to another and another connection. Friends, it's all about relationships.

There is an interconnectedness amongst most community leadership. Once you get into this, you learn how to "get things done around here." It is helpful to know people. If you want some voice, you have to be friends and make connections.

You cannot form connections with too many people. You can connect to the "obvious" leaders, but make sure to connect to the less than obvious leaders as well. At my first church in Kansas City, we had plans to connect the old and new buildings.

Everything was "officially" approved and we were getting ready to start building when the project was shut down by the city council. The local neighborhood association was not pleased with being left out of the conversation and had the project stopped.

This was a hard lesson learned. We should have connected with the homeowners association. This mistake costs us $30,000. Had we spoken with them early on and made friends, it would not have been such a hostile environment. We got it worked out, but it cost time, money and heartache that wasn't necessary.

Are you wondering why there weren't people in the congregation who were a part of or had connections with the neighborhood association? None of the members of that church lived in the neighborhood anymore. I wasn't even living in the neighborhood. The parsonage had been relocated years before. The congregation moved away but still attended church in their "home" neighborhood.

Do not assume your congregation is involved in the community in which your church is located.

Timing is everything. Make time to make friends while the time is right. You need to be friends with decision makers before you need them to make a decision for your benefit.

Remember still, this is not quid pro quo. Don't create relationships for the sole purpose of receiving favors, because there may come a time when you have to take a stand that is quite opposite than the one the leaders want you to take.

Even in small towns, creating these types of relationships is important. However, in our little towns, the owners and managers of our gas stations, dollar stores and local markets do not appear as obvious leaders, but they are. Cultivate friendships with these folks.

Make friends with the people mowing the yards. You never know who's connected into the fabric of a community. I befriended the local yard guy in one of my student churches and we remained friends years later. Upon his

death he left an unexpected sum of money to the church.
You never know what the future might hold.

I would make friends with community decision-makers.

CHAPTER 48

Friend vs. Pastor

There is a difference in knowing your people and knowing your people. This leads me to make a note about one of the great challenges of ministry and in hanging out with your people. One of my mentors told me that my best friendships were going to be clergy. I didn't want that, in fact, I found it a bit depressing. If I had believed that, I would have missed out on some of the deepest friendships of my life with lay people.

That said, I have learned the hard way about managing the role of pastor and friend in the local church. I bear the scars of it and I know others carry scars that I caused.

Perhaps my biggest mistake in ministry happened at my church plant. As the founding pastor, everybody became Bob Farr's friend. That was the only approach to building a church that I knew. We went to Chiefs games, shot potato guns together and planned street parties together. Some of the deepest friendships of my life were built during this time and it was some of the most fun I have had in ministry. All was well and good until our seventh year when I had to start forming deeply important questions in our ministry. Looking back on this moment in my ministry, I am able to call it the "Wednesday Night Massacre" without too much pain. Still, for years I lived with the deep regret that some of the pain exposed that evening, (Ash Wednesday of all days), could have been avoided. It began when a friend and lay leader confessed there was a secret meeting happening at someone's house after Ash Wednesday service. The agenda? Whether or not we really should start the second site I had proposed as part of our vision. A second item of the agenda? We were getting too big.

It was in the midst of this meeting that it hit me. These people see me as their best friend, not their pastor. We were a family. Starting a second site would mean dividing the family they had come to love. It would hurt all our friendships. I had compromised my ability to lead my people into unchartered waters where our relationship would change. In my heart, I knew these changes were for the sake of expanding the kingdom. My friends didn't see it that way. One of them asked a question that pierced my soul: "You're telling me you would chose this decision [to start this new church site] over me?" "Oh no," I thought. "I have this turned around. I have become their friend and buddy who happens to be their pastor instead of their pastor who happens to be their friend and buddy." That may sound like the same thing but it is not. My call to ministry means I have to make a pastoral decision over friendships. I wish I had paid more attention and saw how I had mixed up my role. Instead, I saw 30 people get deeply hurt that evening and leave our church start. They could not imagine me choosing the church and the mission over their preference (and our friendship).

I think this is a great temptation and challenge for pastors. It is hard to strike a balance. People either err on one side or the other. I think most fall into the camp that I am your pastor with strict boundaries which means that you may be friendly but you don't go very deep in relationship. The other side of this challenge is that you lead with I am your friend so you create deep relationships but you will find it difficult to help grow and challenge your people. This is one area of ministry that you have to test and learn from mistakes, keeping in mind that our first General Rule is "Do No Harm." I find Dr. Henry Cloud and Dr. John Townsend's image of boundaries as fences with gates rather than walls a helpful image in managing the complicated role of the pastoral office.12

Keep in mind that big mistakes can occur if you become everybody's friend before you become their pastor. When you have become their friend first and must make a pastoral decision with which they don't agree, you not only go against them, but you run the risk of losing their friendship. You may also cause them to lose their commitment to the Church and ever deeper hurt their relationship with Christ.

12 Henry Cloud and John Townsend, *Boundaries: When to Say Yes, How to Say No to Take Control of Your Life*, Zondervan (1992).

CHAPTER 49

Read the Instructions

I would take time to read the instructions. God gave me a healthy dose of intuition and it has served me well. I'm not much for reading instructions or following directions because I run on instinct most of the time, and it works, most of the time. Still, I have made some major mistakes by not first reading the directions or following instructions.

I can't tell you how many times after putting together toys for our kids on their birthdays or at Christmas, that the toy broke in a couple of days because it was put together "mostly right, but not altogether right." One of the scariest things for me is seeing the words, "Some Assembly Required." The most difficult thing I have ever assembled was the first baby crib. (Since then I have assembled three for kids and grandkids.) There is nothing more frustrating than having to take something apart and start over because you didn't read the instructions first.

In ministry, like in any other job or vocation, intuition is a key gift to have when dealing with people and circumstances. Keep in mind intuition alone is not enough when seeking to understand your congregation and the community. As you do this, start with understanding the community surrounding the church. These are the instructions. Read your instructions. This is your homework. The danger in not doing your homework is that you may not have all the information and cause mistakes that could have been avoided. When these mistakes occur, we tend to get angry with others when we should be angry with ourselves for not preparing well. The result of the homework is an instruction manual for the plans you have for this church. Instead, if you do not follow the directions or read the instructions, you can make a lot of mistakes.

I've heard people say, "I'm going to let the Holy Spirit guide me." John Wesley was all about an informed Holy Spirit. What will the Holy Spirit guide if the spirit has nothing to work with? John Wesley's Quadrilateral (Scripture, Traditions, Reason and Experience) includes factors that Wesley believed helped guide the core of Christian discipleship. When brought together, they bring the individual into an understanding of the Christian faith and practice. Pastors cannot rely solely on their experience or reason, it requires both intuition and doing your homework. Follow the Boy Scout motto, "Be prepared."

When I led church consults and workshops, I found a lot of people winging it. They didn't show up prepared. They didn't do their homework or read their assignments. They weren't ready. They thought that showing up was enough. People always asked, "Does the Healthy Church Initiative work? Do new church starts work?" Yes, but, if you don't work it, it won't work. This is true in your ministry. It's about doing your homework, reading the instructions and following through. Winging it doesn't get the job done very long. My intuition is a gift of God, but it's so much more effective when I confirm it with facts and follow through.

I would take time to read the instructions.

CHAPTER 50

Go Against the Grain

I would go against the grain. I'm a KC Chiefs fan. I love to go to the stadium where 80,000 people gather for a "religious" event. Typically, we sit in the lower bowl of the stadium. So, when the game is over and it's time to get out, you need to go with the flow or risk getting run over. Unfortunately, there have been times when I have needed to go against the flow, upstream, when the other 80,000 people are going the opposite direction. It is extremely difficult and there are many obstacles. In ministry, part of your time and circumstance (not all of it) may cause you to go up the down staircase or go against the grain.

Most of the time, going against the grain is an error in judgment. However, there are a handful of times in which you are called to go against the grain and take a stand that is different from everybody else. However, if you do it too often, it will wear you out and the people will run you over. Do it only when it is most needed or most critical. A system can take only so much of someone pushing against their culture.

There were times when the Prophets had to do it and for them it didn't always turn out well. Peter had to do it in Acts 11. It's not easy going against the grain or going up the down staircase. You have to pay attention, avoid obstacles, weave in and out and take one step at a time. You must determine the things you need to do that catch the least amount of resistance or you will never make it or be heard.

Remember, people resist because they think they are going to lose something. We have a lot of cultural Christianity in our churches. Our churches are filled with very nice, moral people who basically follow the cultural norms of the world (this is how I was raised). They may be one day away from not going to church at all, let alone acting differently than their friends.

Christians need to be more Christ-like, with a biblically based world view and discipleship-minded. Most research studies of American behavior reveal very little difference in behavior between American Christians and American non-Christians. Do we, as Christians, need to mirror the culture of America or change the culture of America? Are you the temperature or the thermostat?

It's been a long time since the church has been counter cultural in regards to having a biblical world view. We have sometimes been counter-cultural politically. We are immersed in our American culture and we don't see a lot of marked differences in behaviors. I grew up in this church / secular culture and thought nothing about it until the American culture casted off its partner called the church, and where we no longer hold any position within the dominate culture. It has left us with a very weak church because we are no longer prompted up by the American culture we were so immersed in.

Now when we occasionally have to go against the grain there is so much push back from our own folks that it makes it very hard to be a force in the secular world. This is because the world has invaded our churches more than our churches have invaded the secular world. Today, we find ourselves lost in the American church. Going up the down staircase seems to be the new normal for most of our churches.

We are in a time when we need to do something different, but use caution. You cannot do it very often or you will get thrown off the staircase. Make no mistake, we are in the business of going up the down staircase. We have to discover our new place within the American culture.

The days of a church-centric culture are gone. When I started my new church in the 1990's you could set up a new church on a visible road, put a good worship show on, have an effective ministry and people would come. Not so today! You have to go get people. You have to go up the down staircase. I've watched our county seat churches in Missouri fade away because we used to be the center of community and everyone knew it and just came. It was the cultural thing to do. Today not so! You have to go up the down staircase. Remember you have the do it carefully or you will simply get run over and make everyone mad. Go up the down staircase anyway!

I would go against the grain.

CHAPTER 51

Be Smart

"Whatever you do in life, surround yourself with smart people."
John Wooden

Surround yourself with good leaders. I learned a long time ago, get the strongest people you can to be around you. I try to hire and get people around me who are smarter than me. Sometimes I've watched pastors do the opposite, I suppose, because they don't want to be shown up. I suppose they are afraid of people who are more talented. Friends, don't be afraid to have people who challenge you and who can make the team stronger. Emotionally secure, strong leaders attract other strong leaders. Strong leaders make you stronger.

Same goes with lay people. Surround yourself with good lay leaders. You're better off with strong leaders every time as long as they are team players. The better work they do the better you look and it saves all kinds of time. Use people who look, act, think and are gifted differently than you. Diversity makes for a better team. We all need a variety of people on the team. Great sports teams have players with different talents. Set a team up with as many strong players as you can and coach them in the direction you need to go to get a win. Then, let them do their work.

Don't micromanage. Turn them loose and let them find their way. Turn loose of the details, but hold tight to the mission, vision and the outcomes. Use benchmark meetings to hold the team to goals but give your people long leashes and let them make mistakes. I don't mind trying and failing. I mind not trying and not showing up. Never turn loose of the mission and vision, but don't worry about the details.

Looking back, I wish I had spent more time recruiting, training and discipling the people around me – my paid and unpaid staff and our laity leading ministries. We spent a lot of time training them in the technical aspects of ministry. I should have spent more time spiritually investing in the people around me. I have always helped people get trained technically in their jobs. I wish I would have spent more time in discipling my team. I should have spent more time being discipled by someone. Talent without discipled grounding doesn't work out well in the ministry of the church.

Hire self-differentiated people. One of the lessons I've learned is to surround myself with emotionally secure leaders with good character. Strong leaders attract other strong leaders. If you are confident, another's success is not a threat to your success.

Jealousy is rampant in our clergy because we are not confident in ourselves. We've cultivated a culture of competition rather than a culture of collaboration. However, we need to learn how to have joy and celebrate in someone else's success.

The sin of competition is my Achilles Heel. My competitive nature was developed on the football field where I found some of my first success. Later in my career, I committed the greatest sin: competition with my very best friend Adam Hamilton. We started our churches at the same time. While my church was successful, his was wildly more successful. That's all I could see and it drove me crazy! Both were wins for the kingdom, right? If somebody wins, everybody wins. Competitiveness comes from a scarcity model. Whoever is first, gets the bigger piece of pie. In ministry, the pie is infinite in God's grace. I don't know if I figured this out until I made it to the judiciary level.

Most of the work I do now is spent helping others be successful and feeling joy in their fruits. I would surround myself with good leaders and take joy in their success and fruitfulness.

I would surround myself with good leaders.

CHAPTER 52

Shift Gears

I would learn when to shift gears. I grew up with a manual transmission car from the 1960's. When learning to drive a vehicle with a manual transmission, without a RPM gauge, you learn to listen and feel for the right time to move to the next gear. If you shift at the wrong time, you can kill the engine or damage something critical. If you shift too late you over-rev the engine. More pastors get into trouble shifting gears (initiating change) than any other single thing. The change might be the right thing to do, but it has to be done right and at the right time. Bringing change to the church is more of an art than science.

In my early days, I had trouble knowing when to make a change because I was not in tune with how and when to do it. On the rare occasion when a church is ready for change, it will meet you at the door. Most churches who say they want change and maybe are expecting a change, will resist it because it is not the change they were anticipating. Most pastors struggle with initiating change or err on the side of no change at all. It's like shifting gears; you have to know when the timing is right. Proceed with caution when people say they want change, lest they get buyer's remorse.

I probably have more regrets over changes I have initiated than anything else I have done. The older I got, the better I got at it. There were many things that needed changing in the churches I served, but I didn't always proceed with right timing and change didn't go as smoothly as it should have. Most churches need lots of shifting. Managing the shifts so you can shift again into the future is important. You have to listen to the engine to know when to shift gears and how fast to shift gears. If you avoid shifting altogether, you cannot get anywhere. If you burn out the clutch you won't get a chance to shift again.

With some changes or shifting, it doesn't matter how well you announce it or how well you do it, the transition will be painful. If the clutch hasn't been used in a while or it's old, it's just going to be noisy. First, you need to estimate how much pain you will have and how quickly it will pass. Then, it's important to know the church's pain tolerance. When is the last time they made a successful shift? Each church has a different tolerance level for pain. There is no universal answer. Like a car, you have to listen and see how they handle it.

In most of my ministry, my habit for change was to jerk the Band-Aid off. This caused me to leave some people behind and hurt. Looking back, I could have gone the other way to get the same change. Sometimes, it's just as well to shift fast. You are always going to leave somebody behind. The harder the shift, the more people you will leave behind. However, the system can only manage so many people being left behind. It will only tolerate so much. How much can your system tolerate?

Make sure you don't make a hard shift for the wrong thing. I have seen people make a hard shift for a change in the worship service only to have that new worship service not be very good and eventually fail. Make sure the shift is worth the pain. Make sure it is done well. Most of the time I didn't regret making a change, what I regretted was not being ready with a better 'new', whatever the 'new' was.

If you're going to transition to something new at your church, if you're going to shift gears, make sure the new ministry is actually worth it. Spend more time making that change a great product or ministry rather than preparing people for the shift. If you want to give your critics some voice, make a change that gets only mediocre results. A bad change will always make it harder the next time. Pay more attention to being ready to do the new thing than announcing the new change. Make sure it's worth it! Learn to shift well.

Make sure you are ready. Change is hard, period. It is an art, not a science. If you're going to change and fail; fail fast. You will have to determine how fast is too fast. How long is too long not to stop? Don't be afraid of change.

I would learn how to shift gears.

Epilogue

"If I would have known" is a reoccurring phrase through this simple book; maybe it should have been the title. When I look back over 40 years of ministry, I am amazed at how much wisdom I gained from either "doing stupid" or making on the job mistakes. I am so thankful of the advance warnings or advice from more experienced colleagues that saved me from the pain of more potential mistakes. "If I had known…"

It's my hope that this book helps pastors and lay leaders today avoid the obvious mistakes that don't look so obvious in the moment. We have all said or heard the phrase, "If I had known what I know now, I would have changed that." Hindsight is always 20/20. Maybe this book will help remind us of the obvious wisdom we need to be more fruitful in our ministry.

Being in ministry is a high calling and privilege. I have loved every moment of my professional ministry as a United Methodist pastor. Indeed, I also know the burdens, bruises, pain, sorrow and long hours that go along with the privilege.

It's my prayer these 54 simple bits of wisdom will lessen the burden, heighten the joy of and strengthen your ministry.

Bishop Bob Farr

Other books from
Market Square Books

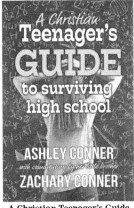

**A Christian Teenager's Guide
To Surviving High School**
Ashley Connor

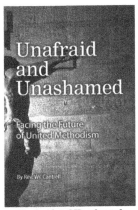

Unafraid and Unashamed
Facing the Future of United Methodism
Wil Cantrell

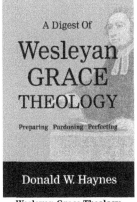

Wesleyan Grace Theology
A Digest of Wesleyan Grace Theology
Donald W. Haynes

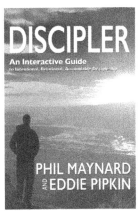

Discipler
An Interactive Guide
Phil Maynard and Eddie Pipkin

IMPACT!
Kay Kotan
and Blake Bradford

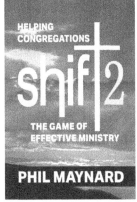

**Helping Congregations Shift 2
the Game of Effective Ministry**
Phil Maynard

marketsquarebooks.com

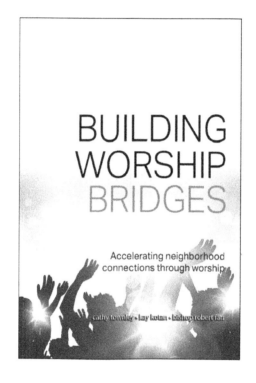

Building Worship Bridges

Cathy Townley, Kay Kotan,
and Bishop Robert Farr